Pocket Guide to
CAMBRIDGE

Published by the Automobile Association,
Fanum House, Basingstoke, Hampshire RG21 2EA

C000079406

Editor: Rebecca Snelling
Copy Editor: Karin Fancett
Illustrations: Alan Roe
Editorial Contributors: Sue Bryan
(City Walks), Mac Dowdy (Buildings
through the Ages), Arthur Harradine
(Cambridgeshire Fenland, A Historic
City, University and College Life
through the Centuries, Gothic
Magnificence), Diana & Lionel
Munby (City Centre: Places to Visit,
The Backs and other Open Spaces),
Honour Ridout (Famous People).

Directory compiled by
Karin Fancett

Maps produced by the Cartographic
Department of the Automobile
Association

Filmset by Vantage Photosetting Co
Ltd, Eastleigh and London, England

**Printed and bound in Great Britain
by** Purnell Book Production Limited,
member of the BPCC Group

The contents of this publication are
believed correct at the time of
printing. Nevertheless, the
Publishers cannot accept
responsibility for errors or omissions,
or for changes in details given

© The Automobile Association
1988

All rights reserved. No part of this
publication may be reproduced,
stored in a retrieval system or
transmitted in any form or by any
means – electronic, mechanical,
photocopying, recording or
otherwise – unless the written
permission of the Publisher has been
given beforehand

ISBN 0 86145 671 8
AA Reference 53455

Produced and distributed in the
United Kingdom by the Publishing
Division of the Automobile
Association, Fanum House,
Basingstoke, Hampshire, RG21 2EA

Contents

Introduction

This compact little book contains everything a visitor will want to know about Cambridge. Designed for easy reference, the guide is divided into four sections, each packed with detailed information which will help readers discover the charm and beauty of this ancient university town.

It is almost impossible to select just a few of the highlights of a visit to the city, but for many people they would include a tour of some of the colleges with their splendid buildings and fascinating connections with famous names. Others may prefer to wander round the city's numerous open spaces or take a leisurely punt along the Backs. Yet others may want to absorb some of Cambridge's great culture; perhaps a visit to the Fitzwilliam Museum or a browse in a few of the city's many bookshops. Read the feature articles to whet your appetite, then use the alphabetical gazetteer section to discover more details of the places you want to visit or the walks section to plan a tour round some of the main attractions.

Within these pages there is also a considerable amount of practical information, plus a street map of the city centre showing places of interest, making this handy book an ideal guide to the city.

About this Book

Cambridge Pocket Guide, designed to be the complete guide for tourist or resident, contains the following sections.

City Plan   A large-scale map of the city centre, with a street index and places of interest clearly marked.

Features   Written by local experts, these introductory articles cover subjects of special importance in the city – from its history and beautiful buildings to the desolate charm of the surrounding fenland and the impact of the University and its students over the centuries.

Places to Visit   Here places of interest, listed alphabetically, are described in detail. Each entry includes the street name, so it can easily be located on the street plan on page 6. For opening times and practical information refer to the Directory.

City Walks   Six walks, with step-by-step route directions, have been carefully planned to take in the best of the city. A clear, easy-to-follow map accompanies each walk. The chief places of interest along the way are described in the text, and these are keyed to the maps by numbers.

Directory   Fifteen pages packed with useful information grouped into sections (see page 77). All you need to know about where to eat and stay, recreation, shops, sports and services, plus useful addresses and opening times for all the places of interest described in the book.

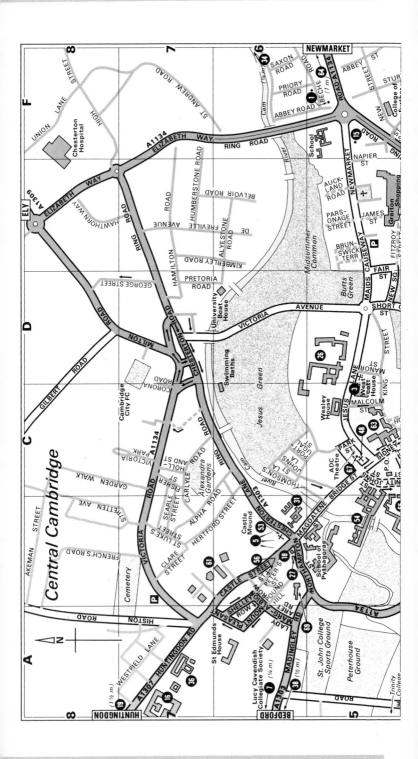

Central Cambridge

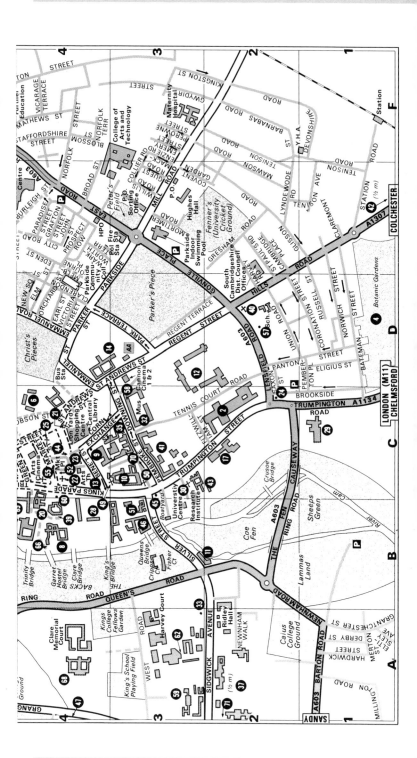

Key to Places of Interest

Key to Town Plan

AA Recommended roads	
Other roads	
Restricted roads	
Buildings of interest	Gallery
Churches	†
Car parks	P
Parks and open spaces	
AA Service Centre	AA

Street Index and Grid Reference

Central Cambridge

Emmanuel Road	D4-D5	Orchard Street	D4-E4
Emmanuel Street	C4-D4	Panton Street	D1-D2
Fair Street	D5-E5	Paradise Street	E4
Fisher Street	C7	Parker Street	D4
Fitzroy Street	E5	Parkside Mill Road	
Fitzwilliam Street	C2-C3		D4-D3-E4-E3-F3-F2
French's Road	B7-B8	Park Street	C5
Garden Walk	C7-C8	Park Terrace	D3-D4
Gilbert Road	C8-D8	Parsonage Street	E5
Glisson Road	E1-E2-E3	Pemberton Place	C1-D1
Gonville Place	D2-D3-E3	Pembroke Street	C3
Grafton Street	E4	Perowne Street	F3
Grange Road	A3-A4-A5-A6	Portugal Street	C6
Grantchester Street	A1	Pound Hill	B6
Green Street	C4-C5	Pretoria Road	D6-D7
Gresham Road	E2	Prospect Row	E4
Guest Road	E3	Queens Road	B5-A5-A4-B4-B3
Gwydir Street	F2-F3-F4	Regent Street	D2-D3
Hamilton Road	D7-E7-F7	Russell Street	D1-E1
Hardwick Street	A1	Saxon Road	F6
Harvey Road	D2-E2	Searle Street	B7-C7
Hertford Street	B7-B6-C6	Shelley Row	A6-B6
High Street	E8-F8	Short Street	D5
Hills Road	D2-E2-E1	Sidgwick Avenue	A2-B2-B3
Histon Road	A7-A8-B8	Sidney Street	C4-C5
Hobson Street	C4-C5	Silver Street	B3-C3
Holland Street	C7	Staffordshire Street	F4
Humberstone Road	E7-F7	St Andrew's Road	F6-F7-F8
Huntingdon Road	A7	St Andrew's Street	C4-D4-D3
James Street	E5	Station Road	E1-F1
Jesus Lane	C5-D5	St Barnabas Road	F2
John Street	E4	St John's Lane	C6
Kimberley Road	E6-E7	St John's Street	C5
King's Parade	C4-C3	St Luke's Street	B7
King Street	C4-C5-D5	St Paul's Road	D2-E2
Kingston Street	F2-F3	St Peter's Street	B6
Lady Margaret Road	A6	Stretten Avenue	B7-B8-C8
Lensfield Road	C2-D2	Sturton Street	F3-F4-F5
Lyndewode Road	E2-F2	Tennis Court Road	C3-C2-D2
Mackenzie Road	E3-F3	Tenison Avenue	E1-E2
Madingley Road	A6-B6-B5	Tenison Avenue	E2-F2
Magdalene Street	B6-B5-C5	Tenison Road	E1-F1-F2
Malcolm Street	C5	The Fen Causeway	B2-C2
Manor Street	D5	Thompson's Lane	C6
Maids Causeway	D5-E5	Trinity Street	C4-C5
Market Street	C4	Trumpington Road	C1-C2
Mawson Road	E2-F2-F3	Trumpington Street	C2-C3
Melbourne Place	D4-E4	Union Road	D1-D2
Merton Street	A1	Union Lane	F8
Millington Road	A1	Vicarage Terrace	F4
Milton Road	D7-D8-E8	Victoria Avenue	D5-D6-D7
Mortimer Road	E3	Victoria Road	A7-B7-C7-D7
Mount Pleasant	A6-A7	Victoria Street	D4
Napier Street	E5	Warkworth Terrace	E3-E4
Newmarket Road	E5-F5	Westfield Lane	A7-A8
Newnham Road	A1-A2-B1-B2	Willis Road	E3
New Square	D4		
New Square	D5		
New Street	F5		
Norfolk Street	E4-F4		
Norfolk Terrace	F4		
Northampton Street	B5-B6		
Norwich Street	D1-E1	© The Automobile Association 1987	

© The Automobile Association 1987

FEATURES • FEATURES • FEATURES • FEA
FEATURES • FEATURES • FEATURES • FEAT
FEATURES • FEATURES • FEATURES • FEATURES • FEA
ATURES • FEATURES • FEATURES • FEATURES • FEATU
RES • FEATURES • FEATURES • FEATURES • FEATURES •
S • FEATURES • FEATURES • FEATURES • FEATURES • FE
FEATURES • FEATURES • FEATURES • FEATURES • FEATU
ATURES • FEATURES • FEATURES • FEATURES • FEATUR
RES • FEATURES • FEATURES • FEATURES • FEATURES •
TURES • FEATURES • FEATURES • FEATURES • FEATURES
FEATURES • FEATURES • FEATURES • FEATURES • FEAT
ATURES • FEATURES • FEATURES • FEATURES • FEATUR
TURES • FEATURES • FEATURES • FEATURES • FEATU
S • FEATURES • FEATURES • FEATURES • FEATURES • FEATU

AA

Pocket Guide to
CAMBRIDGE

FEATURES • FEATURES

Events in Cambridge

*T*he residents of Cambridge often reckon to
be able to tell the time of year by the
concentration of student-propelled bicycles on
King's Parade and the nationality of visiting
tourists. Inevitably the 'student' events are
concentrated in the six or seven months of term-
time, but Cambridge has something happening
all year round, with most events open to students,
townspeople and visitors alike. The listing below
is by month, but some dates vary a little from year
to year, so exact timing should be checked with
the Tourist Information Centre.

JANUARY
Linking the old year and the new is the annual Christmas
Pantomime at the Arts Theatre. Lent Term begins around
the middle of the month.

FEBRUARY
This is the month for the first intercollege rowing races, or
'Lents'. About 15 boats at a time line up, each a boat-
length-and-a-half behind the next. The idea is to catch up
with, or 'bump', the boat in front and in so doing take
their place in the league. Also held in February or early
March is Rag Week—a mid-term chance for students
to let their hair down by performing stunts and
organising events for charity.

MARCH
No sooner do the students seem to have arrived back,
than it is vacation time again! By going away, however,
they may well miss some of the magnificent displays of
daffodils and crocuses to be seen on the Backs at this
time of year.

UNIVERSITY TERM NAMES

Lent – January – March
Easter – April – June
Michaelmas –
October – December

COLLEGES COMPETING IN THE 'MAY BUMPS'

APRIL

Easter usually heralds the start of the main tourist season in Cambridge. The punts are taken out of winter storage, and the tourist guides brush up on their dates and facts. On Midsummer Common the Fun Fair arrives for the first of its several visits during the year, and soon after Easter the students are back again for the new term.

MAY

The Easter Term means exams for most students, so tours around the colleges are somewhat limited to provide peace and quiet for study. However, there is still plenty going on, with the Cambridge Rowing Regatta mid month and singing by St John's College Choir from the chapel tower on Ascension Day. The latter is a comparatively recent custom, introduced in 1904 by Dr Rootham, the college organist and choir master.

JUNE

Despite its name, 'May Week' occurs in early June, once the exams are over. It can be a social extravaganza (for those who have the money and the time!) with May Balls, plays in the college gardens, concerts and, of course, the traditional punting to Grantchester for breakfast. As well as watching elegant and sometimes not so elegant punting, riverside spectators can also listen to the singing of madrigals on the river from the Backs, or cheer on the teams in the 'May Bumps'. Like the 'Lents' earlier in the year, these are held on the stretch of the River Cam between Bait's Bite Lock, Milton, and Stourbridge Common.

Concurrent with 'May Week' and running for a fortnight, is the annual Footlights Revue at the Arts Theatre which has provided a debut for many of those well known in the entertainment world today.

At the end of the month, Midsummer Fair is held on the common of this name. Formerly called the Pot Fair,

'THE BUMPS'

These intercollege rowing races originated in 1826 when boats from Trinity and St John's colleges competed. In 1827 the University Boat Club was established, and by 1832 19 crews took part.

because of the quantities of china sold there, this fair traces its origins back to the 13th century. Also at the end of the month, on the last or penultimate Friday and Saturday, the General Admission to Degrees (or Degree Ceremony) is held. Go to the Senate House, at the junction of King's Parade and Market Street, to see the students and dons in their richly trimmed gowns parade past.

JULY
In mid July the city, as opposed to the University, holds its own festival, the Cambridge Festival. This starts with a carnival fair followed by fireworks on Parker's Piece, and during the two weeks of the Festival there are classical and popular music concerts, many theatrical events (including street theatre), films, international folk dancing displays, a marathon and the city 'Bumps'.

On the last weekend of the Festival, sometimes in early August, the Cambridge Folk Festival is held. This popular event attracts big names from the folk world as well as many excellent local performers. The major concerts take place in the open-air parkland setting of Cherry Hinton Hall, though there are several large marquees for wet-weather use and for the numerous smaller events.

AUGUST
August is a fairly quiet month for organised events in Cambridge with many residents as well as students being away on holiday. At the end of the month, on August Bank Holiday, the Leisure Fair is held. This gives local clubs and societies a chance to publicise themselves and attract new members for the coming year.

SEPTEMBER
At the beginning of September, or sometimes in late August, the Cambridge Fun Run is held to raise money for charities as well as to provide exercise for the participants. Another September event is the Autumn Regatta which is held around the middle of the month.

OCTOBER
October, like April, is a time of changing populations. New students, or 'Freshers', as well as those returning for another year arrive for the Michaelmas Term, while the numbers of tourists dwindle and the punts are once again put away.

NOVEMBER
On Midsummer Common the Fun Fair arrives during the first week of November ready for Bonfire Night. This is celebrated on the common with a grand bonfire and firework display. Later on in the month, the Christmas lights go up in the city centre.

DECEMBER
Michaelmas Term ends, but King's College and its Choir School continue their preparation for the Festival of Nine Lessons and Carols to be held on Christmas Eve. Admission is free, but long queues form for this event which brings the Cambridge year to a close.

Cambridgeshire Fenland

T *he word 'Fen' may suggest an image of a
cold, damp, foggy, flat and waterlogged
area without a single redeeming feature. While
this is undoubtedly one side of the picture, the
fenlands nevertheless have a very special charm of
their own. There are few places in England where
an uninterrupted 180-degree view can be
obtained, and the sight of large clouds sailing
across a vast expanse of blue above the Fens is an
unforgettable experience. Indeed, Rupert Brooke
was so impressed that, in his poem* **The Old
Vicarage, Grantchester,** *he wrote:*

> **. . . I only know that you may lie
> Day long and watch the Cambridge sky.**

FENLAND VEGETATION

Even the small pockets of
traditional fenland remaining,
such as Wicken Fen, have
been modified by man.
Sedges would be mown for
thatching and litter for animal
bedding, resulting in a rich
mosaic of sedges, reeds and
grasses. Nowadays, woody
shrubs tend to encroach on
the sedge beds, and this 'carr'
vegetation has to be removed
in order to encourage the
sedges.

THE PREHISTORY OF THE FENS

Until 10,000 years ago Great Britain was part of the
continental mainland of Europe whose major river was
the Rhine. The river flowed through land now submerged
beneath the North Sea into the ocean south-west of
Norway. In turn, the rivers Ouse, Nene and Welland
drained large areas of what is now eastern England and
emptied their waters into the Rhine.

Some 8,000 years BC the last Ice Age ended and rising
temperatures meant that huge quantities of melted ice
poured into the world's oceans. This led to the raising of
the sea-level, and the consequent inundation of vast
areas of land. As a result of the flooding, an area of some
1,300 square miles stretching from Cambridge in the
south to Lincoln, and from King's Lynn in the east to
Peterborough, was partly submerged. Cycles of flooding
and drying out followed, leading to the formation of the
fenland of today.

For centuries at a time the fenland would be flooded,
but then the area would become drier and support pine
and birch trees, shrubs, reeds and grasses. Then, once
again the sea would overflow and the trees and shrubs
would die and rot away. It was this decaying vegetation
which laid down the beds of peat, often in excess of 60 ft
deep, which provide such rich and fertile agricultural
land today.

THE FENS

THE ROMANS

When the Romans came to Britain in the 1st century AD their engineers attempted to reclaim parts of the flooded fenland by straightening and deepening rivers and waterways and raising river banks to allow more water to be carried to the sea. The Romans were successful in recovering a few thousand acres of pasture-land, but following the withdrawal of the Legions in the 5th century AD, the native Britons allowed the waterways to silt up and the river banks to collapse, and once more the land returned to bog.

RELIGIOUS ISOLATION

ST ETHELDREDA

An unwelcome marriage led to Etheldreda fleeing to the refuge of Ely, protected by the flooded fens. Here she established a monastic community for both men and women and ruled it for four years. After her death in 679 she was venerated as a saint, and pilgrims visited her shrine.

For the next 500 years the fenland was practically a separate country from the rest of Britain, shunned by 'right thinking people'. This inhospitable land became a haven for religious zealots such as St Guthlac who arrived in the 7th century to set up an oratory. At about the same time St Etheldreda founded the religious house which later became Ely Cathedral. Many other religious houses sprang up in the Fens, including those at Peterborough and Thorney. These played their part in fen drainage as each reclaimed from the waters as much land as possible so that the monastery's estates could be extended.

St Guthlac, in his writings, describes his struggles with 'fearsome giants, with twisted faces and necks: wild staring eyes, foul breath and fire in their throats'. Today this seems a wild exaggeration—but is it? The wet, unhealthy surroundings of the fenland led to frequent occurrences of malaria (or ague) as well as rheumatic and respiratory disorders. There is an old fenland saying:

> *Poppy tea and opium pills*
> *Is the cure for fenland ills*

Did Guthlac seek to ease his miseries with the local medicines? If so, perhaps he did 'see' the giants of which he wrote.

ELY CATHEDRAL

THE NORMANS

With the Norman invasion of England in 1066 came further attempts at draining the Fens. The drainage was undertaken partly because the Normans did not like to see such large areas of land lying idle when they could be used for grazing and cultivation. They were also keen to defeat Hereward the Wake, a local Saxon leader, who had refused to accept Norman rule and with a band of like-minded supporters had withdrawn to Ely. At that time Ely was simply a large island standing slightly higher than the surrounding marsh, and it could only be approached by people who knew their way across the waters. The Prior of Ely gave reluctant shelter to Hereward's knights, and from the fastness of Ely they raided the surrounding countryside.

William the Conqueror was not a man to accept such opposition, and by bargaining with the monks of Ely he was able to land troops on the island and defeat the insurgents. In 1081 he sent 86-year-old Prior Simeon to plan and build a new cathedral at Ely. Fortunately Simeon lived to be 100 and saw both the north and south transepts take shape.

The Normans dredged and widened rivers and rebuilt

river banks, adding several thousand acres of useful land to the cathedral estates. All labour was manual, of course, and the silting up of the channels was a continuing problem; rivers changed their course, rivers 'disappeared' completely, and periodic 'drownings' often changed the face of the countryside beyond all recognition.

THE ADVENTURERS AND THE UNDERTAKERS

A serious attempt at draining the Fens was started in the 1620s and 1630s when Charles I, under pressure from local landowners, took a long and serious look at the problem. Around this time also, two types of entrepreneurs, the 'Adventurers' and the 'Undertakers', came on the scene. The former were men willing to risk money in schemes for drainage in return for a percentage of the land recovered. The latter were the contractors who actually carried out the work.

The most famous of the Adventurers was the 4th Duke of Bedford, and it was he who, in 1630, employed the Dutch engineer Cornelius Vermuyden to construct an artificial river some 20 miles long, terminating in a sluice at Denver which prevented sea water flowing up the channel and causing flooding. This proved successful to a limited extent and in 1653 a new channel was cut running parallel to the Duke's channel and some half a mile away. These two rivers, the Old Bedford and the New Bedford, with their straight courses are an unmistakable feature on any map of the Fens.

The more successful the Adventurers were in reclaiming land, the more problems they created, for as the water level dropped the spongy peat dried out and the level of the land sunk, until thousands of acres lay well below the rivers and natural gravitational drainage was impossible. Again Dutch ideas were imported and hundreds of windmills were constructed. In the 19th

WATER PUMP . WICKEN FEN

FENLAND FLOODING

Despite advances in technology over the centuries, the Fens are still liable to flooding. In 1947 the heavy rain and snowfalls during the winter resulted in the flooding of over 60,000 acres of land.

century these began to be replaced by steam engines (the first was installed by John Rennie the Younger in 1818), and by 1850 only 70 such engines were coping with the drainage which had previously required 500 or so windmills.

The final stage of fen drainage which led to the recovery of some 600,000 acres of land began in the 20th century when the steam pumping stations were replaced by oil and later electrically powered pumps. From then onwards the water level could be accurately controlled by switches which brought the pumps into operation automatically, obviating the need for constant manning. But drainage is still vital with so much of the area below sea-level; if all the electric pumps were switched off it is calculated that within a few days the sea would reclaim most of the land of the Fens.

THE FEN DWELLERS

The draining of the Fens was by no means universally popular; the Adventurers and landowners stood to gain, but the Fen dwellers saw it merely as a reduction of the waters from which they earned a precarious living by fishing, eeling and wildfowling. From time to time groups of the Fenmen known as the Fen Tigers rioted and destroyed the work carried out by the Undertakers so as to delay the drainage. The University authorities at Cambridge also opposed the drainage, claiming that their members would have nowhere to hunt and fish for relaxation, and consequently that their health would suffer.

THE FENS TODAY

The viability of the agricultural economy in the Fens is nowadays uncertain. The 60 ft-deep peat beds which provided such rich agricultural land have now shrunk in many places to only 4 or 5 ft. 'Fen Blows', strong and persistent winds which, particularly in spring, strip off top-soil, seeds and fertiliser, add to the problems. Shrinkage also leads to house-building problems on the recovered land, and even houses built on piled foundations still tend to need periodic structural repair.

However, while it is still there, the dark, rich, peat soil provides some of the best agricultural land in England. Wheat, barley, sugar beet, potatoes and carrots are the main crops grown, but fruit, salad vegetables and flowers are also produced. Bulbs are an important crop in certain parts of the Fens, and indeed bulb growing has been so successful that a large proportion of the bulbs grown are sold to the Netherlands.

Very little traditional fenland now remains, the best-known area being Wicken Fen about 10 miles north-east of Cambridge. This is managed as a nature reserve by the National Trust and is popular with naturalists who come to look at the birds and insects as well as the plants. Sites such as the Ouse Washes, where the land between the Old and New Bedford Rivers is seasonally flooded, also provide vital habitats for wildfowl and other birds. Large flocks of ducks, geese and swans can be seen here in winter, but as the ground dries out in spring and summer, species such as black-tailed godwit, lapwing and ruff are amongst the attractions.

MUTE SWAN COBS

A Historic City

*F*or many people the name 'Cambridge'
conjures up a picture of an ancient
university around which a town has grown. The
truth is different; Cambridge was a small
prosperous town 1,000 years before the 'coming
of the clerks'.

EARLY SETTLEMENT

In the 1st century AD the Romans built a road between
their fortified towns at Colchester and Chester, which
forded the river now known as the Cam very close to the
site of the present-day Magdalene Street Bridge in
Cambridge. The higher land to the north (Castle Hill)
provided an ideal site for a fort from which to defend the
river crossing. Around the fort a small civilian settlement
grew.

The small town prospered under the Romans, but
when the Legions were withdrawn from Britain early in
the 5th century AD, it declined rapidly and for a time the
settlement was almost deserted.

The Roman name for the town is not known for
certain, though it may have been *Camboritum*. Other
early records give the name as *Grantabryce* (with a
variety of spellings), then *Grauntbryce* and *Cauntbridge*.
By the 15th century, however, the present-day names for
town and river, Cambridge and the Cam, were in use.

AFTER THE ROMANS

The year AD450 saw an invasion of England by the Saxons
and Jutes, Germanic tribes from the Rhine Valley area.
They came to raid and rob, but stayed on to farm and
settle in East Anglia. Some early Saxons occupied the site
of the old Roman fort at Cambridge, but others started
building on the gravel beds which rose above the
marshes south of the river. A second settlement grew up

SAXONS

here (now the Bene't Street and Market Square area). The name *Lorthburg* or *Lurtheburg* has been given to this village, based on old records which refer to Lortberg Lane in the middle of the settlement.

THE DANES

In the 6th and 7th centuries AD East Anglia was overrun by the Danes and Norsemen from Scandinavia. There followed two centuries of conflict between the English and the new invaders (who were seeking to expand their lands), which ended in 878 when King Alfred defeated the Danes at Ethendune and imposed the Treaty of Wedmore. This treaty effectively confined the Danes to a part of eastern England known as the Danelaw.

The Danes were a seafaring and trading nation, and saw that Cambridge would make an ideal inland port. They built a wooden bridge over the river in about AD750 and established quays on the eastern bank of the Cam between their 'Great Bridge' (at Magdalene Street) and the Silver Street area. Trade goods were brought across the North Sea and offloaded at Lynn (King's Lynn) from where they were transported inland along the rivers Ouse and Cam. These river communications, together with road links (two ancient Roman roads, *Via Devana* and Akeman Street, crossed close to the port area) , enabled Cambridge to become a wealthy town. Most early buildings were made of wood, but in the early 11th century the citizens were prosperous enough to build a stone tower for the Church of St Bene't.

Because the southern village, *Lorthburg*, was closer to the quays than the older town, it soon became the dominant settlement. It was here that a market-place was established, and later the guild and municipal offices. Eventually, however, the two settlements merged into one another.

NORMAN AND MEDIEVAL CAMBRIDGE

Soon after the Norman invasion of England in 1066, William the Conqueror built a wooden motte and bailey castle on the site of the Roman fort at Castle Hill. This was built as a headquarters to control the local population and suppress any revolt from Hereward the Wake and his 'Islanders' at Ely (see page 16), and it is doubtful whether it was ever used as a royal residence.

William's great survey of England, the *Domesday Book* of 1086, showed Cambridge to be a flourishing and important commercial centre with about 400 houses. The Normans encouraged the town's development, and much building took place. The 'Round Church' and the School of Pythagoras, home of the town's first mayor, are two buildings dating from this period (see page 35).

The reign of William II (or Rufus) saw the establishment of the first religious house in the town. An Augustinian monastery was founded in 1092 on the site of today's St Giles' Church at the Castle Street/Chesterton Lane junction. Other denominations soon followed and the religious communities were granted various rights to hold annual fairs, the fees and dues from which supported the house.

In this way Stourbridge Fair, held on the common of that name on the north-east outskirts of the town, came

COAT OF ARMS

Cambridge's coat of arms, granted in 1575, incorporates a bridge and boats, emphasising the importance of river trade in the town's history.

THE PEASANTS' REVOLT

to play a major role in the development of trade in Cambridge. In 1211 King John granted the fair to the Hospital for Lepers, the chapel of which still stands on the Newmarket Road (A45). The proximity of the fairground to the river encouraged merchants from the Continent to trade at Stourbridge, and it rapidly became the largest fair in Europe. It declined in importance in the 18th century and was ended by royal decree in 1933, but its memory is preserved in John Bunyan's *Vanity Fair* which is based on the excesses of the fair.

The origins of the University are probably closely tied to the religious houses and fairs, as monks would have been attracted to the town to preach and teach. However, the date usually given for the foundation of the University is 1209, the year when a group of students, escaping from riots in Oxford, set themselves up in Cambridge (see page 24).

TOWN AND UNIVERSITY
By the late 14th century the University had become a powerful force in Cambridge and, although the first scholars had been made welcome, the townspeople had developed a deep-rooted hatred of the University and its members. The townspeople's complaint was that although the town had held a Royal Charter since 1100, which had been confirmed by King John in 1205, their elected mayor had to swear an oath to maintain the rights and privileges of the University and to yield precedence to the Vice-Chancellor at all times.

The Peasants' Revolt of 1381 saw at least one college plundered by the townsmen who then compelled the Vice-Chancellor to sign away all the privileges and rights that the University held. However, the Bishop of Norwich, with armed troops, entered Cambridge, put down the riots and hanged the five ringleaders. Richard II then restored all the University's rights and privileges and punished the town heavily. It was not until the 19th century that the University eventually gave up many of its rights over the town, and disputes between 'Town and Gown' flared up periodically over the intervening 500 years.

CAMBRIDGE AND ROYALTY

Although it has seldom been at the centre of national affairs, a number of monarchs have visited the town over the years, and on at least one occasion (in the late 14th century) a parliament was held there. In 1553 it was the setting for the proclamation of Lady Jane Grey as Queen of England. However, the Duke of Northumberland, then Chancellor of the University, who made the proclamation did not realise that Mary Tudor, Henry VIII's daughter, was at nearby Sawston Hall. The following day Mary Tudor was proclaimed Queen in London, and although the Duke himself then proclaimed Mary in Cambridge, he was still arrested and executed.

In the 17th century Cambridge again played a major role in national events. The teaching of 16th-century Cambridge churchmen such as Latimer, Ridley and Cranmer led to the rise of the Commonwealth Party and the subsequent beheading of Charles I. Oliver Cromwell, sometime student of Sidney Sussex College, and a Member of Parliament for Cambridge, became the Lord Protector of England. Cambridge commanded the crossing point of routes between East Anglia and the Midlands, and so the town became the Headquarters of the Eastern Counties Association, an armed force set up to defend the area against the King's Army. Cromwell strengthened the Norman castle with stone bought by Clare College for a rebuilding scheme. At the same time he demolished all the bridges over the River Cam except for the Great Bridge. Despite Cambridge's importance in the Commonwealth the University was largely Royalist, and the restoration of the monarch in 1660 was celebrated with wine flowing from the Market Square fountain.

17th- AND 18th-CENTURY DEVELOPMENTS

In the mid 17th century road links with London were improved and the first regular coach service between the towns started in 1653. The year 1724 saw the passing of an Act of Parliament which authorised Turnpike Trusts to collect a fee from road users for the maintenance of the highway. The engraved stone marking the point at which the Godmanchester turnpike road ended can still be seen on the wall of No 8 Castle Street.

This period also saw the development of various social amenities. Early in the 17th century Dr Stephen Perse left money in his will to found a free school to educate 100 boys and to build almshouses. Both are still in use though on new sites. A century and a half later, in 1766, the famous teaching hospital named after Dr John Addenbrooke, a Fellow of St Catharine's College, was opened.

ENGRAVED SIGN IN
CASTLE STREET
CAMBRIDGE.

THE 19th AND 20th CENTURIES

The Reform Act of 1832 put an end to many municipal excesses. It followed an enquiry by a Royal Commission which found Cambridge to be one of the most corrupt boroughs in England. The affairs of 20,000 people were controlled by only 158 freemen with voting rights, who apparently had no hesitation in spending £1,300 on dinners at the same time as providing only £480 for council services and road repairs.

The Victorian period saw the arrival of the railway in

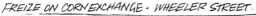

FREIZE ON CORN EXCHANGE · WHEELER STREET.

Cambridge, with the consequent development of more speedy communications. However, the University authorities decreed that the station must be a suitable distance away from the colleges, hence its location in the south-east of the town a couple of miles away from the city centre.

Later in the 19th century a large Corn Exchange was constructed for the county's farmers, and the town also opened a free public library and reading room.

Like most other towns, Cambridge lost many of its young men in World War I. Even so, there was much unemployment in the town in the 1920s. Government funds brought some relief in allowing the construction of bridges—a footbridge over the Cam in the north-west of the city linking Pretoria Road with Midsummer Common, and a series of bridges across Coe Fen and Sheep's Green from Trumpington Road to Newnham. The road across these bridges, Fen Causeway, was expected to be a waste of money as no one would need to use it. Today, however, it is one of the city's busiest roads.

A boundary expansion took place in 1934 when large areas of Trumpington and Cherry Hinton were added to the town, increasing the area to more than 10,000 acres. Between the wars four major new schools were built to accommodate the increasing numbers of children, evening classes for adults became popular, and two new branch libraries were built in the suburbs.

World War II caused the number of students in the town to diminish rapidly as they were called up, but the vacated college accommodation was soon filled by trainees for the Forces, mainly RAF. A certain amount of damage to property was caused by bombing, and a number of people were killed, but fortunately Cambridge never became a military target in spite of its surrounding aerodromes and 6,000 trainee airmen.

The period since the war has seen a steady rise in industry and building in the city. Much of the industry has been in the scientific and hi-tech fields and more Science and Business Parks are being opened on the outskirts of the city. These enable small firms to set up in pleasant surroundings and to make use of the scientific and other specialised skills available within the University departments.

Observant readers may have noted that despite the title of this article, Cambridge has generally been referred to as a 'town' rather than a 'city'. This is because despite its size (with a population of over 100,000) the town of Cambridge was only elevated to city status in 1951.

POPULATION NUMBERS

In the late 16th century the town of Cambridge had a population (excluding students) of around 5,000 people. By 1801 this had nearly doubled to over 9,000. The 19th century saw a rapid increase: to 20,000 by the 1830s and to nearly 40,000 by the turn of the century. In this century the population has again doubled to around 100,000.

University and College Life through the Centuries

*B*eautiful college buildings and peaceful courtyards, traditions and privileges are the hallmarks of the University of Cambridge, but today this ancient seat of learning—an amalgamation of colleges, faculties, libraries and museums—is also a leading scientific research centre.

THE EARLY YEARS

The origin of the University in Cambridge is unknown, but it is generally considered to date from 1209, when a group of students who had been driven out of Oxford by serious rioting came to Cambridge to continue their studies. They may have arrived with the intention of setting up a 'School', but it is rather more likely that they came to one already established.

A 'University' in its simplest form was a body of learned men gathered together for the purpose of teaching. These men, the 'Masters', would only allow people to teach once they were satisfied as to their abilities. The licence to teach was known as a 'Degree', and degree holders were permitted to teach in any part of the country. Following a Papal Bull of 1318, Cambridge was declared a *studium generale* or place of general education, which meant that degree holders could teach in any Christian country.

The early University had no money of its own, nor did it own property. The principal study was theology, requiring much of the scholars' time to be spent in devotions, and local churches provided for this need. Religious houses and churches were also used as lecture rooms and for University ceremonies.

THE CHANCELLOR'S COURT

In the early days of the University its Head, or Chancellor, would hold a court at which he would try all cases involving students. The result might be imprisonment, expulsion or excommunication.

HOSTELS

Unless a scholar studying at Cambridge was a member of a religious house, it was necessary for him to provide for his own board and lodgings, and usually he would reside with a family in town. This caused certain problems: the young students (usually only 14 or 15 years old) were frequently accused of being ill-disciplined, and the landlords often saw students as a ready source of income and overcharged them.

As a result it became increasingly common for Masters and their scholars to band together to purchase or hire a local house in which they lived a communal life. The larger of these houses became known as 'hostels', and at times there were as many as 27 hostels in the town. However, such hostels did not solve the problems of youths of scholastic ability who lacked the money necessary to stay in Cambridge for seven years in order to reach Degree standard. The late 13th and 14th centuries saw the emergence of benefactors who, for the salvation of their souls, were willing to provide charitable funds to support such scholars.

THE COLLEGES

In 1280 Hugh de Balsham, the Bishop of Ely, decided to install a group of student monks in Cambridge to enable them to study and attend public lectures. He was no doubt prompted by the establishment, 16 years earlier, of Merton College, a house for maintained scholars in Oxford. The young monks from Ely were housed at the Hospital of St John in Cambridge, a charitable foundation where old and infirm men were nursed by some of the older Ely monks. Unfortunately, the young monks were unable to live peaceably with the older brothers, and in 1284 Balsham acquired two tenements outside the southern boundary of the town and installed his scholars there. The tithes of St Peter's Church were used to support his college, and when Balsham died two years later he left money which enabled the college to buy land and erect a hall, St Peter's College or Peterhouse.

As this college was maintained by the Bishop of Ely, only monks from Ely could live there. However, Balsham's foundation encouraged others, and in the 70 years following the establishment of Peterhouse five new collegiate foundations appeared. There then followed a space of almost 100 years, a time of plague and public unrest, before 1441 when Henry VI founded his college dedicated as 'The King's College of the Blessed Virgin and St Nicholas' and now known as King's College. Another nine colleges arose by 1594, but then there was another lull until around 1800 when Downing College was founded.

Today there are 31 colleges established in Cambridge, including three which were founded for ladies. The first of these (Girton) started life at Hitchin in 1869 and transferred to its Huntingdon Road site in 1872. In the late 1960s some of the men's colleges began to accept women, and this led to a rise in the number of female students in the University. Women now comprise 39 per cent of the total student population of around 12,000.

COURTS OR QUADS?

In Cambridge the college buildings surround areas known as courts. In Oxford they would be called quads!

COAT OF ARMS - GATE TO KING'S COLLEGE

ADMINISTRATION OF THE UNIVERSITY AND COLLEGES

As stated already, the University is defined as the 'Chancellor, Masters and Scholars', but the decision-making or executive power is in the hands of the Regent House. This body consists of all residential Masters of Art (or MAs)—essentially the teaching and research staff of the University—and is too large for effective administration. University business is therefore first discussed in the Council of the Senate (whose members are elected from the Regent House), and its decisions and recommendations are then passed on to the Regent House for final approval. *Ad hoc* committees are formed to advise the Council on specialised matters, and experts in the appropriate field are invited to serve on such committees.

The head of the University, or Chancellor, is usually a person holding high public office (the present incumbent is Prince Philip), and the day-to-day business is conducted by the Vice-Chancellor who is the head of one of the colleges. The post of Vice-Chancellor is held for two years.

The governing body of a college consists of the Master and Fellows (the senior teaching and administrative staff), but here, too, power is vested in the College Council, selected by vote from the college's residential MAs.

FINANCE

The University is financed in part by Government grant, in part by money from national and international research agencies, and in part by payments levied on the colleges based on an elaborate system of taxation. Money also comes from endowments, some ancient and some modern. Industries and commerce may, in addition, finance research and even endow Professorships, but despite this only the utmost frugality on the part of the Board of Finance allows so much research to be carried on in Cambridge.

The colleges receive no state aid and are funded by bequests and student fees. Some, having owned land and property over many centuries, are very rich; others are much poorer. However, there is a good relationship between all the colleges, the wealthier ones contributing money to the 'University Chest' on which the less wealthy colleges can draw for special items of expenditure.

ROWING ON THE CAM.

THE FACULTIES

In early days the University provided a degree course in two parts which took seven years to complete. The Trivium (first three years of study) included grammar, logic and rhetoric. This was followed by the Quadrivium, with arithmetic, geometry, astronomy and music. New subjects were included in the course of studies from time to time, and particular encouragement to expanding the curriculum was provided by Prince Albert, Chancellor from 1847.

The first endowed Cambridge Professorship (or Chair) was that in Divinity founded by Lady Margaret Beaufort, the mother of Henry VII, in 1502. Since then Chairs have been founded by public benefactors and by past members of the University in many subjects. Around the Professorships, departments, grouped into 20 faculties, have grown. A wide range of subjects are now taught and researched, ranging from physics (where Cambridge has produced many of the famous names of the 20th century—see page 33) to oriental studies, architecture and the history of art, and criminology. Research students are attached to particular departments, but undergraduates, though attending lectures and sitting examinations provided by the University, are supervised and tutored by their colleges.

OTHER UNIVERSITY FACILITIES

In addition to the lecture halls, libraries, laboratories and offices of the departments, the University also administers a number of museums. These are used by the students in connection with their studies but most are also open to the public. Several, including the Museum of Archaeology and Anthropology, the Museum of Zoology, and the Sedgwick Museum of Geology, are to be found in the Downing Street area. Nearby, in Free School Lane, is the Whipple Museum of the History of Science. The department libraries are, like the museums, primarily for students and researchers' use, but the University Library has changing exhibitions of some of its books and organises guided tours on weekday afternoons. Other University facilities include the Botanic Garden and the Fitzwilliam Museum, both well worth a visit (see city gazetteer).

UNIVERSITY SPORTS

Students of old were considered to be at college just to study, and sporting activities were not encouraged. Football and 'such like rowdy games' were frowned upon, and there are references in some University histories to scholars being forbidden to play marbles on the steps of the Senate House. Play acting, circuses and bear baiting required a licence from the Vice-Chancellor if the performance was to be within five miles of the University. But each college had its bowling green, bowls being the only officially approved sport.

Today's students are given every opportunity to take part in a wide range of sports including tennis, rugby, rowing and even tiddly-winks. For some, there may be the chance of a 'Blue', awarded to those representing the University in Oxford versus Cambridge sporting encounters.

THE COLLEGIATE SYSTEM

Each Cambridge college selects its own students and is responsible for its own administration. Each student will have a Supervisor, and their regular meetings, known as tutorials, are regarded as an important aspect of study at Cambridge.

*HENRY VI LECTERN
KING'S COLLEGE*

Gothic Magnificence

*T*he Chapel of King's College is world famous, and each year hundreds of thousands of people visit it and walk beneath its magnificent vaulted ceiling. Millions more know of it through the annual broadcasts of the Festival of Nine Lessons and Carols on Christmas Eve.

THE EARLY DAYS OF THE CHAPEL

The beautiful Gothic building was begun in 1446 by Henry VI who, at the age of 19 years, founded King's College of which the Chapel is a part. The civil strife of the Wars of the Roses slowed down the building of the Chapel, and it was 70 years before even all the walls and roof were complete. Construction took place during the reigns of five monarchs and was finally completed in the middle years of the 16th century.

In 1461, 10 years after the civil war broke out, Henry VI was overthrown. At this time only the first four bays from the east had been completed. The Yorkist Kings, Edward IV and Richard III, carried on with the Chapel to the original design and at the time of Richard's defeat at the Battle of Bosworth Field in 1485 seven bays were completed to roof height, four of which were roofed enabling the eastern end to be used.

Building work came almost to a standstill in the latter part of the 15th century as to start with the new king, Henry Tudor (Henry VII), took no interest in the Chapel. However, by the beginning of the 16th century its founder, Henry VI, was being regarded as a saint, and Henry Tudor thought that his hold on the Crown might be strengthened by a public display of his support for his predecessor. On St George's Day 1506 he visited Cambridge and gave the sum of £5,000 towards the cost of construction. In addition he undertook to provide sufficient further money to ensure the Chapel's completion. On Henry VII's death in 1509 his executors provided funds for finishing the building, leaving only the furnishings to be provided.

In 1512 the master mason John Wastell was appointed, and he signed a contract to construct a vaulted ceiling at a cost of £100 per bay with a contract time of three years. Wastell's vaulting is of the 'fan' variety, and is breathtaking in its lightness and beauty. Notice that in the Chapel the fans spring from corbels half-way up the wall, whereas in the Ante-Chapel the fans spread from columns with their bases on the floor.

The stone used for the first stage of the Chapel was a white magnesian limestone, transported by water from a quarry near Tadcaster in Yorkshire. Delays in building, and probably financial considerations, led to the Chapel being completed in an oolitic limestone quarried near Northampton. This is a darker rock, and a look at the buttresses on both the north and south sides of the building shows clearly how far work had progressed at the time of Henry VI's overthrow in 1461. The change in stone is most noticeable at the bases of the two western turrets.

SLOW PROGRESS

Henry VI laid the foundation stone of his Chapel on the Feast of St James (25 July) 1446. Finally, after 69 years and four days (29 July 1515), the stonework of the Chapel stood complete.

ADDING THE FINAL TOUCHES

With the walls and roof finished by 1515, the College approached the young Henry VIII for help in furnishing the Chapel. Henry responded by granting money to provide the windows, flooring, organ screen and stalls.

Installation of the windows began in 1515 and continued until 1545, although the west window, depicting the Last Judgement, was not put in until 1879. The medieval windows, in an arrangement known as type and anti-type, depict scenes from the New Testament in the lower half, and related scenes from the Old Testament in the upper sections. A number of designers worked on the windows, the best known being the King's Glaziers, Barnard Flowers and Galyon Hone.

The oak organ screen in fine Renaissance style covered with intricate carvings is a tribute to the wood carver's art. It was constructed before 1536 while Henry VIII was married to Anne Boleyn, and bears the couples' initials, H and A, above the entrance. The choir stalls are of a similar age to the organ screen, although the hoods above and the carvings are of a later period, having been commissioned in 1633. Also of a later date are the screen gates which bear the coat of arms of Charles I and the date 1633.

The first organ was installed in 1606 and was replaced in 1688 by a Renatus Harris organ. This, too, has been enlarged and rebuilt on several occasions.

THE CHAPEL IN THE 20th CENTURY

Fortunately the Chapel survived the ravages of two world wars intact. The windows, probably the best complete collection of medieval windows in the country, were removed to a place of safety before World War II. Their replacement was started in 1948 and it took five years to put back the 1,300 square yards of glass.

The altar piece, the *Adoration of the Magi* by Peter Paul Rubens, was given to the College in 1961 and, some 10 years later, the eastern end of the Chapel was altered by lowering the altar steps so that the Rubens could be displayed to the best advantage. The painting can now be viewed through the organ screen arch from the west end of the Chapel.

THE CHAPEL CHOIR

The choir still consists of 16 boys as ordered by Henry VI but nowadays it is augmented by 14 male voices. Famous past members of the choir include Orlando Gibbons who composed madrigals and motets in the 17th century. The choir boys can often be seen in the afternoon when, dressed in top hats, Eton jackets, striped trousers and gowns, they march in a 'crocodile' from their school to the Chapel for rehearsals or services.

VISITING THE CHAPEL

There is a minimum of unobtrusive low-power electric lighting in the Chapel and Ante-Chapel, but the real glory of the interior can best be appreciated when the candles are lit for the evening service in winter, and the walls and fan-vaulting recede into a shimmer of candle-light. Most of the services in term-time are open to the public; the times are displayed on a notice board in the south porch.

CHAPEL EXHIBITION

The small chapels on the north side of the building house an exhibition of the history and construction of the Chapel. There is also a bookstall which sells postcards, guide books and recordings of the Chapel choir.

CHORISTERS OF KING'S COLLEGE CHAPEL

Famous People

*O*ver the years of its existence the university
at Cambridge has, like any other
university, produced large numbers of people
who have led worthy (though not noteworthy)
lives in such professions as the Church, teaching
and administration. Others have achieved more
lasting fame: as statesmen or martyrs, as scientists
or entertainers.

BISHOP RIDLEY

Nicholas Ridley (c. 1500–1555)
was a student and later
Master at Pembroke College.
He was an ardent Reformer
and in 1550 was made Bishop
of London. However, in 1555,
during the reign of Queen
Mary, he was found guilty of
heresy and on 16 October
was burned with Latimer
opposite Balliol College in
Oxford.

JOHN MILTON

BISHOPS AND COURTIERS

The religious upheavals of the 16th century turned many
Cambridge men into martyrs. Bishop John Fisher, the
great benefactor who had instigated the founding of
Christ's and St John's colleges, was executed in 1535. His
'crime' was to deny the claim asserted by Thomas
Cranmer, that Henry VIII should be head of the Church in
England. Cranmer himself had been a student at Jesus
College, but nearly blighted his career by marrying.
However, his wife died, so Cranmer returned to college,
entered Holy Orders, became the king's chaplain and
finally Archbishop of Canterbury. But in 1556 he died at
the stake in Oxford on a charge of heresy. Shortly before
his death he witnessed the burning at the stake of
Bishops Ridley and Latimer, from Pembroke and Clare
colleges respectively.

Although Cambridge continued to produce
churchmen in large numbers, in the latter part of the
century young aristocrats were also attracted to the
University. Robert Devereux, Earl of Essex and later a
favourite of Queen Elizabeth I, went to Cambridge when
he was only 10 years old. He was placed in the care of the
Master of Trinity College, but nevertheless managed to
spend beyond his means and had to write a contrite
letter to his guardian, Lord Burleigh.

THE PURITANS

Most students, however, came from humbler
backgrounds. Oliver Cromwell's father was a gentleman
of Huntingdon who, in 1616, sent his son to Sidney
Sussex College. Cromwell was a student in Cambridge for
only a year before his father's death necessitated his
return home, but later he became Member of Parliament
for the town and established his Eastern Counties
Association there during the Commonwealth Period. In
1960, a head (almost certainly Cromwell's) was returned
to his old college for reburial, but its exact whereabouts
are kept secret.

John Milton, the great poet, was a student at Christ's
College for seven years from 1625. He found himself at
odds with his more frivolous companions, who
nicknamed him 'The Lady' for his fastidious ways and
smooth face. But he was not without a wry humour.
When the local carrier Thomas Hobson died, Milton's
epitaph for him described Death's pursuit along the
London road.

In the early 17th century, many of Cambridge's
staunch Puritans sailed to New England where they could

worship as they chose. In Cambridge, Massachusetts, they founded their own college, naming it after John Harvard, a benefactor who had recently arrived from Emmanuel College.

PEPYS AND NEWTON

Early in 1651 Samuel Pepys arrived at Magdalene College. His family came from Cottenham, near Cambridge, and some of his kin were officers of the town council. The college records mention Pepys only once, on the occasion when he was 'scandalously overseen in drink'. While a student, he spent some time writing a novel called *Love a Cheat* which in later years he tore up, though marvelling that he could have written so well. But it was as a book collector that Pepys made his lasting contribution to Cambridge, for he left his own superb library and bookcases to Magdalene. His famous shorthand diary, recording daily life in the 1660s, is also housed in the library.

Pepys came to know the most famous scientist ever to study at Cambridge, Isaac Newton. Even as a schoolboy Newton showed an unusual interest in things mechanical and scientific, and at Trinity College he distinguished himself as a mathematician, becoming a Fellow and then Professor of Mathematics. He lived most of his life in Cambridge, and though he was actually at home in Lincolnshire when the famous incident of the falling apple is said to have occurred, the theory of gravity that resulted was written (in Latin) at Trinity. An apple tree by the college gate and a statue in the chapel commemorate him.

THOMAS GRAY AND THE ROPE-LADDER

In the 18th century, Cambridge was renowned, as Byron later put it, for its 'din and drunkenness'. To this world came Thomas Gray, a scrivener's son of refined tastes and quiet but biting wit. Gray decided to stay at Peterhouse, after taking a degree in law, to pursue his own interests in the classics, history and writing poetry. Nowadays he is, of course, best known for his *Elegy Written in a Country Churchyard*. To some of the undergraduates he was a figure of fun and they saw a wonderful opportunity for some sport when Gray had a rope-ladder installed in his top-floor room as a fire escape. On a February night the young men gave a false alarm after, some say, placing a tub of water beneath Gray's window. Whether he tumbled down his ladder into it is not recorded, but Gray was mortally affronted by this prank. When the Master of Peterhouse declined to punish the offenders, Gray removed to Pembroke College.

18th-CENTURY POLITICIANS

Another person connected with Pembroke was William Pitt (the Younger) who came up to the college as a boy of 14. Though so young and suffering ill health, Pitt's academic ability was recognised and he studied enthusiastically with his tutor until he left college in 1779. Within a year he had a seat in Parliament, and in the general election of 1784 he became Member of Parliament for Cambridge University. He had already, at

JOHN HARVARD (1607–1638)

In 1637, the Cambridge-educated English clergyman, John Harvard, emigrated to Massachusetts. Although he died shortly afterwards of consumption, he achieved immortality because of his gift of over 300 books and £779 to the proposed college later named after him.

THOMAS GRAY

the age of 24, been made Britain's youngest Prime
Minister. After his death in 1806 he was commemorated
in Cambridge by the University Press (Pitt) Building in
Trumpington Street and a statue at Pembroke College.

A close friend and colleague of Pitt was William
Wilberforce, his contemporary at St John's College.
Wilberforce, who came from Hull, was an able and very
sociable young man but even he thought it odd that his
tutor should invite him straightaway to an evening's
gambling. However, the combination of hard work and
fun seemed to suit Wilberforce very well and was a way
of life he continued into adulthood. From Cambridge he
went into Parliament and there took up the case against
slavery.

'A GLIMPSE OF CAM'

William Wordsworth, from distant Cumberland, was also
a student at St John's College. He described later his
arrival in Cambridge in 1787, how he

> . . . caught,
> While crossing Magdalene Bridge, a glimpse of Cam
> And at the Hoop alighted, famous inn.

His rooms were over the college kitchens and there he
could hear not only the domestic hubbub but also the
more dignified tones of 'Trinity's loquacious clock'. For a
while, he said, he gave up the solitariness he had enjoyed
as a boy in the Lakeland fells, and joined in the bustle of
undergraduate life. He even admitted getting drunk while
toasting Milton's memory in the poet's old room.

A year or two later Samuel Taylor Coleridge arrived at
Jesus College. Although the lives of the two poets
became bound up together, they met only after leaving
Cambridge. Coleridge was in some ways a misfit in the
University. Although a good classical student and writer
he was, apparently, too interested in current affairs, too
curious and not good enough at mathematics. Failing to
achieve his ambitions, he ran away from Cambridge and
enlisted in the Army as Silas Tompkins Comberbache. He
was eventually found out and returned to Cambridge,
but could not settle and left without a degree.

LORD BYRON

BYRON

The ultimate representative of unreformed Cambridge, of
the system at its worst, must be George Lord Byron. As
we have seen, he recognised Cambridge's shortcomings
and exploited them for his own enjoyment. College
Fellows were themselves often idle or drunk but many of
them pursued any aristocrat or man of influence who
might offer them employment elsewhere. Lords, even
undergraduate lords, were given many privileges. Byron
arrived at Trinity, in 1805, an overweight, slightly lame
youth rejoicing in his new independence. He
immediately ordered three dozen bottles of wine and
arranged for his horse to be stabled in town. Byron
delighted in taunting the Fellows, and on finding the
college forbade the keeping of dogs within the grounds
acquired a bear cub which he paraded through the
courts quite legitimately. When asked about the bear's
future he replied 'he shall sit for a fellowship'. Despite this
sort of behaviour and long absences in London, Byron
was still awarded the customary degree.

EVANGELISTS AND APOSTLES

While Byron's experience epitomised the old order, in the late 18th and early 19th centuries the energies of those who wished to reform Cambridge were being released. A greater sobriety amongst the undergraduates was encouraged by the evangelical vicar at Holy Trinity Church. Charles Simeon of King's College had barely graduated before obtaining the living and setting about preaching a more inspired gospel than was usual at the time. He particularly aimed to help the many other undergraduates destined for the Church, and his tea-parties became famous. There students could discuss the doctrines, practice and teaching of Christianity in a way not provided for by the University. Simeon was at Holy Trinity from 1782 till his death in 1836. He was buried in King's College Chapel.

University reform was a very slow process and when Alfred Tennyson arrived in Cambridge in 1828 he could still observe sycophantic Fellows flattering young noblemen. Tennyson's first observations on Cambridge were not complimentary. He nevertheless found congenial friends and became one of the early associates of a society called the Apostles. Membership was by invitation and was extended only to those seen to be intellectually gifted and with open, inquiring minds. A measure of secrecy was observed about all the Society's affairs, and this is still so today. Tennyson was a published poet before going to Cambridge and there he continued to write, which cost him his degree.

EVOLUTION

In the same year that Tennyson went up to Trinity, Charles Darwin entered Christ's College. His father hoped he would become a clergyman, thinking his interest in natural history was not likely to lead to a profession. However, Cambridge had professors of Botany and of Geology and they encouraged Darwin's interests. Professor Henslow recommended Darwin for the post of naturalist on the *Beagle*, a ship setting off to survey South America and the Pacific. Thus Darwin began the work that resulted in *The Origin of Species*.

By the time Darwin's own sons had grown up, Cambridge was teaching and examining degree courses in the sciences. George, Horace and Francis Darwin all studied at Trinity and remained in Cambridge. They were of the generation that was at last allowed to marry without relinquishing fellowships, and they all brought up their families in Cambridge. In time, George's son Charles became Master of Christ's, his grandfather's college.

THE CAVENDISH LABORATORY

The decision in the early 1870s to set up a degree course in experimental physics was hotly debated, but the point was won by the progressives and the University's Chancellor, the Duke of Devonshire (whose family name was Cavendish), paid for the laboratory. After 1874 when the Cavendish Laboratory was completed, physicists became some of the University's most famous members. They included students who had graduated at other universities, such as Ernest Rutherford from New Zealand. He came to the Laboratory in 1895 to work

LORD TENNYSON

under J J Thomson on electromagnetic waves, and in 1908 won the Nobel Prize for Chemistry. After several years spent teaching in other universities, he returned to Cambridge as Cavendish Professor in 1919, and during the 1920s and 1930s headed research into the splitting of the atom and the behaviour of its components.

Other Cambridge Nobel Prize winners include father and son W H and W L Bragg who studied X-rays and crystal structures and won the Physics Prize in 1915, and E D Adrian who won the Physiology and Medicine Prize in 1932. Francis Crick and James Watson (together with Maurice Wilkins) won the Physiology and Medicine Prize in 1962 for their work on the structure of DNA, the genetic code which determines heredity, and Sir Nevill Mott who was Cavendish Professor between 1954 and 1971 was one of the joint winners of the Physics Prize in 1977.

'GRANTCHESTER, AH GRANTCHESTER'

One of King's College's most well-known past students is Rupert Brooke. Brooke's name is, for most people, linked with Grantchester, a village two miles south of Cambridge. Like many students he had no sympathy with Cambridge town, and in the poem *The Old Vicarage, Grantchester*, wrote:

For Cambridge people rarely smile,
Being urban, squat and packed with guile

However, he loved the 'holy quiet' of Grantchester, with the overshadowed river, the bees and their honey in his landlord's garden and the silent church clock. At King's College he enjoyed a range of student activities, political, dramatic and literary, and he was elected an Apostle. After graduating he lodged in Grantchester, first at the Orchard then at the Old Vicarage, while working for a fellowship. He was an attractive but sometimes unconventional figure who shocked the worthies of Grantchester by appearing in public view barefoot. His death early in World War I epitomised the loss of a generation of promising young men. His name is inscribed with the war dead on the village memorial and in King's College Chapel.

THE FOOTLIGHTS

Since the revival of amateur dramatics amongst the students about a century ago, Cambridge has produced a succession of performers known through stage, screen, radio and television. Jack and Claude Hulbert were members of the Footlights Dramatic Club in the 1910s, Richard Murdoch in 1925 and Jimmy Edwards in 1939. Club members in the 1920s included Norman Hartnell and Cecil Beaton, whose talents for design were used in the Club's productions. Another drama group, The Mummers, was founded in 1929 by Alastair Cook, writer of the *Letters from America*. However, he was less successful at talent-spotting, for he told James Mason, then at Magdalene College, to stick to architecture. In the 1950s and 1960s Cambridge (and Oxford) graduates led new movements in entertainment and humour, and Jonathan Miller, Peter Cook, David Frost, Eleanor Bron and many, many, others became known to everyone with a television set.

THE BLOOMSBURY GROUP

Several young men, who were to form a lasting association known to the outside world as the Bloomsbury Group, arrived at Trinity at the end of the 19th century. They included the Stephens brothers, Thoby and Adrian, Leonard Woolf (who married the Stephens' sister Virginia), Clive Bell and Lytton Strachey.

Buildings through the Ages

*C*ambridge can provide a complete history of *English architecture. The oldest surviving building dates back to before the Norman Conquest of 1066 and each succeeding style of architecture can be found somewhere within the town and university areas of the city. Modern architecture is well represented too, if not universally well-liked, and much of it is in the international prize-winning bracket.*

THE OLDER BUILDINGS

The oldest building still standing in Cambridge is the tower of St Bene't's Church in Bene't Street, just off King's Parade. Thought to have been built a little before 1050, it displays, both inside and out, the proportions and features of pre-Conquest, or Saxon, building. The walls are very thick at the base, getting a little thinner each time as they rise through three stages. The stones at each corner form an irregular pattern known as 'long and short work', and the main window openings have somewhat crudely carved round-headed arches cut into massive blocks of stone supported by sturdy baluster shafts. Most of the church was heavily restored in the 19th century, and the aisles were rebuilt at this time.

The Church of the Holy Sepulchre, more commonly known as the Round Church, stands towards the town end of Bridge Street. This is one of only four surviving round churches in the country. The circular nave and aisle were built in the first half of the 12th century together with a small rectangular chancel which was enlarged in the 13th century and again in the 15th century. In 1841 the eminent architect Anthony Salvin was highly praised for his restoration of the church; today many people think that it was very much overdone. However, there is much original and restored work to admire and enjoy inside the building. The most interesting original Norman work is the lower level of the nave where eight solid columns with roll-moulded arches link with the rib-vaulted ceiling of the aisles.

All the other medieval churches in the city have interesting features which record the constant remodelling that was practised from the 11th through to the 16th centuries. Today we are so used to accepting these buildings as we find them, that it is difficult to appreciate how revolutionary the introduction of new styles would have been at the time.

The most visually interesting of the older secular buildings is the School of Pythagoras in St John's College. It is one of those great rarities—a two-storeyed stone-built Norman house. The older, round-headed windows indicate a late 12th-century age. The shafts and capitals are in the transitional fashion developing from the Norman into the Early English style. Entrance to the original building would have been on the first floor by an outside staircase to a door at the east gable end, but by the 14th century doorways had been inserted at ground level.

SCHOOL OF PYTHAGORAS

Cambridge has more timber-framed buildings than are at first obvious, and many of the smaller buildings still to be seen in the city centre were constructed in this way. Most of them hide behind remodelled façades of brick-casing or stuccoed rendering, but there are some that reveal all. Bridge Street, between the bridge and the Round Church, proudly boasts some very fine buildings. Bridge House, which has a passage-way leading through to a multi-storey car park, is double-jettied, which means that the two upper floors project. The timber revealed is expansive and expensive.

There are three other timber-framed buildings in the city also worth closer inspection, namely the Folk Museum at the bottom of Castle Street, west of the river, the Varsity Restaurant in St Andrew's Street, and the Little Rose, a pub opposite the Fitzwilliam Museum in Trumpington Street. All would have been situated outside the main part of medieval Cambridge, although there had for a long time been a settlement in the area around the Folk Museum.

THE FORMER WHITE HORSE INN, BUILT IN THE 16TH CENTURY — NOW THE FOLK MUSEUM

Cloister Court in Queens' College shows both timber and brick construction. Three sides of the court have 15th-century brick; an extremely expensive material in those days. The fourth side confirms the court's picturesque quality with the immaculate timberwork of the President's Gallery. Legend has these timbers coming from ships, but that is most unlikely as it was, and still is, virtually impossible to remodel saltwater-seasoned wood.

King's College Chapel (described in greater detail elsewhere—see page 28) is, of course, the most magnificent example of the ultimate of English Gothic style, the Perpendicular period of the late 15th and early 16th centuries.

17th-CENTURY BUILDINGS

The mid 17th century brought a distinct change of architectural style to England, which, in Cambridge, is reflected in the work of Christopher Wren. Wren's Pembroke College Chapel of 1665 is the earliest of Cambridge's purely classical buildings. Three years later he produced Emmanuel College Chapel, and in 1676 began Trinity College Library (commonly known as the Wren Library), the most visually peaceful of buildings. The Fellows' Building at Christ's College, begun in 1640, the inner ranges of the main court of St Catharine's College, dating to the 1670s, and the Pepys' Building at Magdalene, which was certainly there by 1688 (the date on the façade, 1724, commemorates the arrival of Pepys' library), are other superb secular examples of the period. Clare College by itself provides us with a history of architectural development in the second half of the century. In addition, the way that the light plays on the intriguing patterns of the south wall, when viewed from King's College bridge, is well worth seeing.

18th-CENTURY BUILDINGS

The south side of the Front Court of Emmanuel College is graced with the much-acclaimed Westmorland Building of the first quarter of the century. It is a pleasant enough building but does not have the charm of two smaller contemporary town-houses, Fitzwilliam House (opposite the Fitzwilliam Museum) and Little Trinity (in Jesus Lane), which is a favourite of many people. Little Trinity was remodelled from an early 17th-century house, and the steep pitch of roof, the parapet, the symmetrical distribution of sash-windows, and the excellent door-casing, all combine to produce a splendid looking façade.

About the same time that these domestic houses were being built, James Gibbs was designing more formal buildings for the University and for King's College. The Senate House, in King's Parade opposite Great St Mary's Church, presents an elegant catalogue of classical features and decoration and the cornice beneath the balustraded parapet is a wonder of craftsmanship. Gibbs' Fellows' Building at King's can be admired from both the town and the river sides of the college. It is a plain, very restrained building that contrasts with the elaborate Gothic decoration of its neighbours.

DOORWAY, SENATE HOUSE PASSAGE

19th-CENTURY BUILDINGS

The latter years of the previous century had been very quiet in Cambridge with little expansion occurring. The 19th century proved a complete contrast and a time of great vitality. With the number of undergraduates almost trebling in the first 30 years of the century, many new college buildings were constructed and there is a feast of architecture for the gourmet.

Of all the eminent architects to contribute to the Cambridge scene at this time William Wilkins was the most prolific. Most of his work is in the Gothic Revival style. It can be seen in the New Court at Trinity College, the Second Court at Corpus Christi College, and in many of the buildings around the Great Court of King's College, namely the Screen and Gateway, beside King's Parade, and the Hall Range, opposite the Chapel. In complete contrast is his Greek Revival of 1807 at Downing College with its spread of pavilions within a wide, lawned area. This was the earliest of all university campuses anywhere in the world.

Another piece of Gothic Revival architecture that has inspired followers is the New Building at St John's College. This is a large symmetrical building, surmounted by a tower with a cupola in the Gothic style, with a court enclosed by a screen. It is linked with the older courts by the so-called Bridge of Sighs. All these were built between 1825 and 1831 by Thomas Rickman and Henry Hutchinson. The final choice of 19th-century college building is Alfred Waterhouse's 1870s rebuilding of Tree Court at Gonville and Caius College which has a Belgian or northern French appearance.

To complete the 19th-century selection is one church and one commercial building. George Bodley designed All Saints Church in 1865. It is a very fine and elegant piece of Gothic Revival, set off by its well-proportioned tower and spire. A feature of note is the interior decoration by William Morris. Opposite Petty Cury on Sidney Street is Lloyds Bank Chambers. Alfred Waterhouse with Paul, his son and partner, designed the greater part of it in 1891; the rest dates to 1935. The external mixture of styles leads one into an interior of elaborate Egyptian forms in heavily decorated tiles.

SCHLUMBERGER BUILDING

THE MODERN BUILDINGS

It is very easy to condemn, criticise and complain, and collect a sympathetic ear where recent 20th-century architecture is concerned. When it comes to accepting new design most of us reveal rather conservative traits. We sometimes overlook the fact that all earlier buildings were at one time modern, and that many were very avant-garde in their day.

The big central tower of the 1931–4 University Library by Sir Giles Gilbert Scott dominates the Cambridge skyline. A theme of vertical strips against a less obvious horizontal line dominates the whole building. The pale russet brickwork fades to a muddy grey in most lights giving it an impersonal air. The Sidgwick Site of faculty offices, libraries, lecture rooms and a museum brings together the work of a number of architects. The variety of shapes and materials are linked together by the controlled space between and sometimes beneath the buildings. The problems that hit James Stirling's prize-winning History Faculty, 1964–8, with collapsing cladding, and difficulties with the heating and the ventilation, tend to make people wary of new materials. One can imagine Gillespie, Kidd and Coia's Robinson College, of 1980, maturing in the manner of other and older brick-built colleges; yet, one has doubts about the concrete-clad colleges.

Two of the newer commercial buildings provide similar points of comparison. Anyone driving along the M11 close to Cambridge is bound to see the great marquee-like structure that dominates the High Cross site just off Madingley Road. Completed in 1985 and designed by John Hopkins, the Schlumberger Building has a very temporary look. Despite the sturdy forms of its posts and bracework it looks no more permanent than a circus tent. The teflon-coated glass-fibre of the canopy already shows a canvas-like discolouring. The glass-faced office cabins along the sides seem all ready for container shipment. Nevertheless, despite these criticisms, it is a very exciting piece of architecture. Equally exciting, but with a feeling of reliable permanence, is the Napp Building on the Science Park off Milton Road. This can be seen and approached from the A45 dual-carriageway. Designed by Arthur Erickson and Partners, building began in 1981. It uses sloping buttress-like columns, cast in Spanish dolomite aggregate, and panels of reflective insulated glass. Inside and out the building glows with quality.

CAMBRIDGE ARCHITECTS

Some well-known architects associated with Cambridge buildings are listed below: Christopher Wren (1632–1723), James Gibbs (1682–1754), Thomas Rickman (1776–1841), William Wilkins (1778–1839), Alfred Waterhouse (1830–1905), Giles Gilbert Scott (1880–1960).

The Backs and other Open Spaces

Cambridge is fortunate in the survival of so much green, open space where visitors and residents alike can walk or simply sit and watch the world go by. Many of these areas also have backdrops of fine buildings to delight the eye.

THE BACKS

The lawns and gardens between the River Cam and the colleges, and the river and Queen's Road, are collectively known as the Backs and are, probably, Cambridge's best-known open space. They stretch from St John's College in the north, down to Queens' College in the south. Footpaths weave up and down across the Backs but, especially in summer, the best views can be obtained from a punt on the river. The Backs are also worth visiting in March and April for the displays of spring flowers.

Much of the attraction of the Backs is in the rich variety of architectural styles represented by the buildings bordering the lawns and the river. Starting in the north, St John's College displays the neo-Gothic façade of New Court, together with the 'Bridge of Sighs' which joins the two parts of the college. Then comes Trinity College with Sir Christopher Wren's library, Clare College with its classical south range, and King's College with its Gothic chapel and 'Great Lawn'. Further south still is Queens' College, and here it is the modern buildings, the sympathetic Erasmus Building and the stark, white Cripps Court which face the river.

OTHER RIVERSIDE COMMONS AND GREENS

The Backs are only a part of an arc of open spaces bordering the river, stretching from Stourbridge Common at the north-east of the city to the meadows down towards Grantchester to the south.

Often the names of these open spaces are fascinating and informative. Coe Fen, in the south, for instance, gets its name from the jackdaw, or 'coo' in Old English. The name of the neighbouring Sheep's Green is fairly self-explanatory, while Lammas Land, also in the south-west

ON THE BACKS

part of the city, is so named because it was cleared at Lammas (1 August). These three areas, which are rather more 'rural' than the commons to the north of the city, have a number of nature trails crossing them and are used for grazing cattle and horses.

Where the river curves eastwards in the north of the city it encircles Jesus Green with its avenues of large plane trees and open-air swimming pool. Across Victoria Avenue is Midsummer Common, so-called from the fair held there at midsummer since the 13th century. Further east still along the river is Stourbridge Common, where Stourbridge Fair, 'the largest and most famous fair in all England', was held from King John's reign until the 1930s: Stourbridge was the steer, or ox bridge. Across Newmarket Road is Coldham's Common, the cold 'hamm' meaning meadow.

THE CITY SQUARES

Within the city are a number of more formal open spaces, the largest of which is Parker's Piece. This was named after Edward Parker, a chef at Trinity College, who grazed cattle on the green in readiness for the table. The turrets of the University Arms Hotel in the north-west corner of the square loom over Hobbs' Pavilion, a memorial to the Cambridge cricketer Jack Hobbs who achieved 197 centuries and more than 61,000 runs during his first-class cricket career. The Pavilion, erected in 1928, is now a restaurant specialising in pancakes. Parker's Piece is much used by local sports clubs, as well as being the site for the opening carnival of the Cambridge City Festival, and nearby are other sports facilities, the Kelsey Kerridge Sports Hall and Parkside Swimming Pool, and Fenner's, the University cricket ground.

Other smaller city squares include Christ's Pieces with its trees, flower beds, bowling green and tennis courts, at the back of the Bus Station, and New Square, adjoining it to the east. New Square has terraces of town-houses on three sides, built in the second quarter of the 19th century to a coherent design, but with interesting individual differences. Its charm has been restored now that the car park has gone and the area has been regrassed.

AA

Pocket Guide to CAMBRIDGE

PLACES TO VISIT • PLACES TO VISIT

Abbey House/Barnwell Priory

Abbey Road (off Newmarket Road)

Abbey House occupies part of the site of the old Augustinian Barnwell Priory which was dissolved in 1538. All that remains of the priory is a vaulted chamber known as the Cellarer's Chequer (which may have been part of the kitchen) at the corner of Beche and Priory Roads, and the nearby small 13th-century church of St Andrew the Less which was attached to the priory. By the end of the 16th century stone from the priory was being removed for buildings elsewhere; some was used in the construction of Corpus Christi Chapel.

The house itself, which is privately occupied, is a mixture of timber-framed and brick construction, built in three phases between the late 16th and 18th centuries. On the attractive 'Dutch' west gable, with its altered windows, the date 1678 can be seen.

Addenbrooke's Hospital

Trumpington Street

The old hospital, opposite the Fitzwilliam Museum, was founded and endowed in the 18th century by Dr John Addenbrooke, a Fellow of St Catharine's College. It was reconstructed by Sir Matthew Digby Wyatt in 1863–4, and fragments of the original building were incorporated in the structure. An ugly top storey was later added to the façade.

By the mid 20th century new buildings were urgently needed, and the New Addenbrooke's Hospital was developed on a site to the south of the city. The first buildings were opened by the Queen in 1962. Since then New Addenbrooke's has become a regional hospital and medical school and maintains close connections with the University.

The University bought the site of the Old Hospital in 1986, after it had closed, and proposed to pull the building down. However, local opposition has been considerable and as a result the façade at least may be preserved.

All Saints Church

Jesus Lane

This is one of several disused churches in Cambridge now in the care of the Redundant Churches Fund. It was built in the mid-1860s in Gothic Revival style by George Bodley. William Morris was commissioned to decorate the interior walls and ceilings. In addition there are Minton tiles in the chancel, and the east window has figures designed by Burne-Jones, Ford Madox Brown and Morris.

Barnwell Priory

See Abbey House

Botanic Garden

The original University Botanic Garden, founded in 1762 by Dr Richard Walker, Vice-Master of Trinity College, was used mainly for the study of medicinal plants. It was sited on five acres of land off Free School Lane, later to be built over to form the New Museums Site.

Although land for a new garden in the south of the town was purchased in 1831, it was another 15 years before the gardens were officially opened. A plaque on the large lime tree near the Trumpington Road entrance commemorates the date, 9 November 1846. The new 40-acre site, bordered by Hills Road, Bateman Street and Trumpington Road, was not all developed immediately, but early features include most of the large trees, the systematic beds with the plants grouped according to their botanical relationships, the lake and rock garden, and the glasshouses. The eastern half of the garden site was used as allotments until after World War II, when the bequest left by Reginald Cory enabled the more recent features to be developed.

Today the attractions include the chronological bed, planted according to the date of introduction of the plants, the scented garden, and the conservation garden which contains species rare in their natural habitat in Britain.

Bridge Street

The east side of Bridge Street, between Magdalene Bridge and the Round Church, is one of the most successful examples of the renewal of old buildings in Cambridge. A number of derelict properties were saved from demolition, restored and re-opened as shops, while a modern office block and a multi-storey car park (in Park Street) were incorporated unobtrusively behind.

Bridges

During its passage through Cambridge the River Cam is crossed by a railway, five public highways, eight public footbridges, and six private college bridges. It was first bridged, before 875, near Magdalene College; the present 1823 bridge, strengthened in the 1970s, is an unusual three-pin cast-iron arch. Silver Street has had one or more bridges since the 14th century—indeed, at one time, the road was known as Small Bridges Street. The newer bridges are further out from the city centre. Fen Causeway was built in 1924–8 to provide work for the unemployed, and Elizabeth Way Bridge in 1971 to take pressure off the 1890 iron Victoria Avenue Bridge to its west.

The oldest surviving college bridge, Clare Bridge (1638–40), is much more graceful than James Essex's Trinity Bridge (1764–5), to its north, or William Wilkins' King's Bridge (1819), to its south.

The original wooden Queens' Bridge (now known as the 'Mathematical Bridge') designed by undergraduate W Etheridge, was completed in 1750. The myth that it was constructed by interlocking straight pieces of timber in such a way that no nails or bolts were necessary is probably untrue. The present copy, dating from 1902, does have bolts, and resulted in another myth that students were used to take the earlier bridge to pieces but were unable (or too inebriated) to put it back together again. The northernmost college bridges belong to St John's: the covered bridge by Henry Hutchinson, which resembles the Venetian 'Bridge of Sighs',

built in 1831 to connect the older courts with New Court, and Sir Christopher Wren's attractive bridge of 1709–12 (known as the Kitchen Bridge or Old Bridge) which is situated a few yards to the south.

Since the 16th century there has been a public right of way over the Backs by successive Garret Hostel bridges, the present one being constructed in 1960. All the other public footbridges date from the late 19th or 20th centuries.

Caius College

See Gonville and Caius College

Cambridge Castle

Castle Street

All that remains of the Norman castle which once dominated Cambridge is an earth mound in the grounds of the modern Shire Hall. However, it is worth climbing the mound on a fine day for the excellent view of Cambridge it affords. The castle, built for William the Conqueror in the early days of his reign, was a wooden motte and bailey construction. In the 13th century it was rebuilt in stone by Edward I, but by the 16th century it had fallen into disrepair. Queen Mary I is said to have granted some of the stone from the castle to the Huddleston family of Sawston Hall who had sheltered her in 1553 (as she fled from Lady Jane Grey's supporters), and whose hall had, as a result, been burnt by local Protestants.

MATHEMATICAL BRIDGE

CHRIST'S COLLEGE GATE

Christ's College

St Andrew's Street

This college is attractive in itself and interesting for its associations, with John Milton (see page 30), Charles Darwin (see page 33) and Field-Marshal Smuts (the Afrikaner soldier-statesman) among its more famous graduates. The college, founded in the 1440s on the site of what is now King's College Chapel, was originally known as God's House. However, when Henry VI wanted the land for his own King's College, it was moved to its present position. In 1505 Lady Margaret Beaufort (mother of Henry VII) renamed it Christ's College. She also provided funds for a college nurse, a country shelter from plague, and clean surplices. Lady Margaret's arms, over the main gate, are similar to those over the gate of her other college, St John's.

The First Court of Christ's College was completed in 1511, incorporating in the gatehouse wing earlier buildings of God's House. Originally of clunch and red brick, the façades were re-faced in stone during the 18th century. The hall was altered and panelled by James Essex in the mid 18th century and later (between 1876 and 1879) was entirely rebuilt, using the old materials, by George Gilbert Scott. There are many early features in the chapel and notable stained-glass in its north windows, some of which may have come from the old God's House. The east window of 1912 is thought to depict Henry VII as well as Lady Margaret Beaufort and John Fisher (her Confessor),

with the college itself in the background.

A very attractive Fellows' Building was added in the 1640s on the far side of Second Court. Behind the building is the Fellows' Garden with its 17th-century college 'Bath' and 18th-century summer-house. Also in the garden is Milton's mulberry tree. Sometimes said to have been planted by the poet, it is more likely to be one of 300 mulberries introduced by the college in 1608 (coincidentally the year of Milton's birth) for James I, who was keen to produce English silk.

At the far northern side of the college site, backing onto King Street, is an architecturally interesting, pyramid-like building designed by Denys Lasdun.

Churchill College

Storey's Way

This national memorial to Sir Winston Churchill, founded in the early 1960s, was intended particularly for students studying engineering, mathematics and the natural sciences—a visit by Churchill to Massachusetts Institute of Technology led to a wish to encourage this area of education. It has flats for married students and was the first college in which senior members sat in the dining hall together with junior members instead of on a raised dais (known as the 'High Table') at one end.

The college buildings consist of a series of three-storey open blocks, designed by Richard Sheppard, and built mainly of stone-coloured bricks and slabs of concrete patterned by wood shuttering. Between the buildings are modern sculptures by artists such as Henry Moore and Barbara Hepworth.

General de Gaulle gave the college a Jean Lurçat tapestry which is displayed in the library named after Brendan Bracken, a faithful political friend of Sir Winston. Another part of the college's library, the post-graduate reading room, is named after Ernest Bevin, the outstanding wartime Minister of Labour and National Service, and post-war Labour Party Foreign Secretary.

Clare College

Trinity Lane

This was the first college in which undergraduates and Fellows lived together as a community—the idea of the effective foundress, Lady Elizabeth de Clare who, in 1338, took over the earlier University Hall and re-endowed it. A fire in 1521 led to rebuilding between 1523 and 1535. However, by the early 17th century the buildings were in disrepair and the college was almost completely rebuilt in the 17th and 18th centuries.

There are two distinct parts to the college, which is divided by Queen's Road. The Old Court off Trinity Lane is very much of one style, although the building of it was delayed by the Civil War of the 1640s and took 130 years (1638–1769). The early buildings include the chapel, which extends outside the court towards the lane and has an altar-piece by Cipriani. A footpath, past Clare's gardens and over the lovely 17th-century bridge, leads to Memorial Court, designed by Sir Giles Gilbert Scott in memory of the members of Clare who were killed in World War I. The new library, opened in 1986, was built in the middle of this court.

Among the roll-call of college Fellows have been Bishop Latimer, martyred in Mary I's reign, and Nicholas Ferrar, founder of the Little Gidding religious community in Huntingdonshire—which devoted itself to prayer and fine bookbinding. Famous undergraduates of the college include Charles Marquess Cornwallis, who surrendered to the rebellious North American colonists at Yorktown in 1781.

Corn Exchange, The

Wheeler Street

The Corn Exchange, behind the Guildhall, and across the street from the Tourist Information Centre, was built in 1874 from local brick and iron roof ribs shipped from Antwerp. Its name explains its original use; it once housed about 130 stands where the county's farmers could trade their produce. When, in the 1950s, it was no longer needed for this purpose, it served for many years as a public hall, being used for roller-skating, dances, beer festivals and other events. It was renovated in the early 1980s and at the end of 1986 was re-opened as a modern 1,450-seat concert hall with excellent acoustics. The cleaned brickwork reveals colours and shapes of surprising variety. The building's origins are indicated by the stone panels either side of the main entrance as well as in the frieze of farming activities inside.

Corpus Christi College

Trumpington Street

Originally known as Bene't College, and standing between the churches of St Bene't and St Botolph, Corpus is unique among Cambridge colleges in that it was founded, in 1352, by two town guilds rather than by a monarch or other rich benefactor. Old Court, a lovely 14th-century enclosed court and the earliest surviving in Cambridge, is at the northern, Bene't Street end of the college. The buildings are linked by a gallery to St Bene't's Church, which served as the college chapel until 1579.

New Court or Second Court, of 1823–7, is joined to Old Court by a passage-way in the middle of the south range of buildings which contains the hall. William Wilkins designed New Court in the Gothic Revival style, a remarkable contrast with his earlier Downing College buildings. Wilkins' chapel, on the east side, replaced an earlier one on the same site which had been built in the 16th century largely at the expense of Sir Nicholas Bacon, father of Francis Bacon and a Corpus graduate. Queen Elizabeth I and Sir Francis Drake also contributed to the costs of this earlier chapel. The library, on the south side of the court, contains a priceless collection of manuscripts and early printed books salvaged at the Dissolution of the Monasteries by Matthew Parker, Master of the college between 1544 and 1553 and later Archbishop of Canterbury. Parker is commemorated by a statue outside the chapel, and also commemorated, by a plaque, is the Elizabethan dramatist Christopher Marlowe who was a student at the college.

CORPUS CHRISTI COLLEGE

Darwin College

Silver Street

Darwin College, which consists of a line of houses between the street and the River Cam, joined together to make a terrace, does not immediately look like a Cambridge college. The modern architecture linking the old houses can be clearly seen from Silver Street; the picturesque river side is best viewed from the end of Mill Lane. In the centre of the range is Newnham Grange, joined to a little island by a bridge. The Grange was, from 1885, the home of George Darwin, son of Charles Darwin, famous author of *The Origin of Species*. Darwin College was founded in 1964 to cater for research students and senior University members who otherwise had no effective college links.

Downing College

Regent Street

The view into the college from the entrance off Regent Street is all space, light and proportion. A grass area, larger even than Trinity's Great Court, is flanked by stone buildings on only three sides. The neo-Grecian style seems appropriate for an institution intentionally different in many ways from the older colleges. It was the first new foundation since the 16th century, and later had the first married Fellows, as well as the first endowed professorships in Law and Mathematics.

William Wilkins, at the age of 24, won a competition to design the new college. His plan was to space out the college buildings instead of making enclosed courts, thus effectively creating the first campus—10 years before Jefferson built the University of Virginia campus at Charlottesville. The endowment for the college came from Sir George Downing, who died in 1749, but building was long delayed by a bitter and costly lawsuit over his will—so costly that money ran short before building was completed. The east and west ranges, in classical style, were built between 1807 and 1821 and more was added in 1874–6, following Wilkins' plans. His intention was to have a large entrance gate in the northern area, but when building was finally resumed in the 1930s and 1950s this was completely filled in.

Famous people connected with Downing College include Frederick William Maitland, a historical genius who was a Downing Professor of the Laws of England in the 1880s, and Dr Alan Howard, who has financed a recent college building, and devised the widely known Cambridge Diet.

Downing Street sites

On either side of Downing Street are crowded a number of different scientific departments which have always been enormously important in the development of the sciences. Included in the site, with its entrance on Free School Lane, is the Whipple Museum of the History of Science (see page 64).

The northern New Museums Site was developed in the 19th century in an area once occupied by an Augustinian friary, Cambridge's first secondary school—the Perse—and the original 18th-century Botanic Garden. The site was named after the 'new' Museum of Anatomy, opened in 1833. For the last 150 years the area has been crammed tighter and tighter with buildings serving ever-changing scientific purposes. The Cavendish Laboratory of 1874, creation of William Cavendish, Duke of Devonshire and Chancellor of the University, was world famous for the fundamental physics investigated there (see page 33). Great scientific achievements were also made in other departments on the New Museums Site; an example is the work of the biochemist Sir Frederick Gowland Hopkins who 'discovered' vitamins.

After World War II the Cavendish Laboratory moved into a new building west of Cambridge off the Madingley Road, an area envisaged as a future science campus, and the Chemistry Laboratory, too, moved out to Lensfield Road. But many of the science departments are still based on the New Museums Site, with new departments, such as aerial photography, computing, and audio-visual aids, taking the place of the older ones.

The 'Downing' site to the south of Downing Street was acquired by the University between 1896 and 1902 and filled with new scientific buildings, some departments moving from the older New Museums Site. The buildings facing Downing Street currently house the Department of Earth Sciences and the Faculty of Archaeology and Anthropology, both of which have fascinating museums.

Eagle, The

Bene't Street

This old coaching inn, originally named the Eagle and Child, is entered through an archway from Bene't Street. The courtyard is noteworthy for its first-floor open gallery, dating from around 1800, which is attached to the oldest part of the inn, built some 200 years before. The inn has long been a favourite haunt of students and it was here that many of Crick and Watson's discussions on DNA (see page 34) took place.

Emmanuel College

St Andrew's Street

Built on the site of a Dominican friary, and founded in the 1580s by a leading Elizabethan Puritan, Sir Walter Mildmay, Emmanuel has particular associations for Americans. Out of 100 Cambridge graduates who emigrated to New England before 1646, 35 came from Emmanuel, among them John Harvard who gave his name and his library to the American university. His life is commemorated by a plaque in the chapel.

Front Court together with the inappropriately named New Court was the core of the original college, lying between Emmanuel and St Andrew's Streets. Only the west and east ranges of New Court and the range which divides it from Front Court now remain from the buildings of the 1580s. The old courts include the friary church, transformed into the College Hall and refitted in the late 18th century by the Cambridge architect James Essex Junior who also re-faced the south front of this hall range in ashlar and built the west entrance front.

On entering the college from St Andrew's Street through Essex's range, the building opposite is Sir Christopher Wren's Chapel and Cloister (dating from the 1660s) and, on the right, is the Westmorland Building—largely financed by the 6th Earl of Westmorland and designed by a committee. It was built midway in time between Wren's chapel and Essex's front.

Emmanuel College is fortunate in the space which it has available and is well known for its attractive gardens. Around the lawns and lakes of the Paddock and Chapman's Garden are grouped the college's more modern buildings.

THE EAGLE, BENE'T STREET

Festival Theatre

Newmarket Road

A plain building on the opposite side of the road to the *Cambridge Evening News* office houses a small theatre built in 1814 and originally known as the Theatre Royal. In the 1860s it became a Mission Hall but then was re-opened as the Festival Theatre between the wars. Many future famous actors and actresses including Robert Donat and Flora Robson made their debut here. Despite being closed again in 1934 it still retains most of its early 19th-century interior arrangements although the seating has been removed. Today it is used as a store by its successor, the Arts Theatre, which was founded in 1936.

Fitzwilliam College

Huntingdon Road

Fitzwilliam College began in 1869 as a non-collegiate community founded for men who wished to study but did not want to, or could not afford to, belong to a college. Its first home was a Georgian house opposite the Fitzwilliam Museum in Trumpington Street. In the 1960s Fitzwilliam became a full college and moved into buildings designed by the architect Denys Lasdun. The glass and concrete vault of the present dining hall is particularly striking, as is the college's new block on Storey's Way.

Fitzwilliam Museum

Trumpington Street

The Fitzwilliam is one of the oldest and most remarkable museums in the country, containing some of the best collections of ceramics, paintings, coins, medals and antiquities outside London. Its collections are housed in an imposing temple designed specifically for the purpose by George Basevi in 1834. The museum was eventually opened in 1848, and there have been subsequent additions, the most recent in 1975, when the restaurant and shop were added.

The museum's founder, Richard 7th Viscount Fitzwilliam of Merrion, bequeathed 144 paintings to the University in 1816, along with books, prints and 130 illuminated manuscripts. His portrait as a Cambridge undergraduate in 1764, by Joseph Wright of Derby, hangs in the room at the top of the stairs.

Under the fine Corinthian portico is excellent bold early Victorian plasterwork. The entrance hall, one of the finest of any provincial museum, has the grandeur of a London club, and, indeed, it is the work of Sir Charles Barry, architect of the Reform Club in London. Perhaps he wanted to give an appropriately exclusive air to the museum; when it was first opened it was only available to the 'properly dressed' public on three days of the week. Even members of the University, who could use it at other times of the week, had to be dressed 'in Academical Habit'.

In the **Lower Galleries** are antiquities, ceramics, coins and medals, and armour. At the bottom of the right-hand stairs the Egyptian antiquities rooms contain coffin cases showing the journey of Espawershefi through the Netherworld, protected by the Goddess Nut. Also on display is a rare collection of Egyptian drawings on flakes of limestone. The rooms to the left contain Greek and Roman antiquities: for example, the Roman mosaic fountain niche, and part of a Roman couch, painstakingly restored from fragments by members of the museum's staff. These rooms also contain the magnificent Bacchanalian procession of the Pashley Sarcophagus (c.AD130).

Glass doors lead to the English and Continental ceramics galleries, the Fisher and Glaisher collections—the latter without doubt the best collection of ceramics outside London. Exhibits range from 17th-century English brown-glazed earthenware to fine chinoiserie Meissen, red anchor Chelsea and Victorian Parian figures. The Far Eastern gallery is at the right-hand end of the second pottery gallery: a Ming dynasty buffalo in green jade, until 1900 part of the furnishings of the Winter Palace in Peking and now one of the largest pieces of jade sculpture in Western collections, is one of the highlights here. The room also contains 11th-century Sung dynasty porcelain, as well as later enamelled 18th-century porcelain, some of which was made for export to Europe.

At the other end of the pottery gallery is the armour room, with a German fluted set for both horse and rider, and a fine 16th-century Milanese parade helmet in the form of a lion mask. Two little rooms open off the armour room. That on the left contains coins and medals, including Quentin Matsy's romantic *Erasmus* of 1519. It also contains one of the best small collections of English glass in the country, much from local sources. Arranged in chronological order, running clockwise from the right as you enter, it includes a rare Elizabethan Venetian-style soda glass, probably by Verzelini. The room to the right has medieval illuminated manuscripts, including the Grey Fitzpayn *Book of Hours*, fine Coptic and Byzantine ivories, Gothic carvings, and Elizabethan portrait miniatures, including works by Nicholas Hilliard and Isaac Oliver.

The **Upper Galleries**, devoted primarily to paintings, were laid out in comfortable carpeted and furnished 'state room' manner by Sidney Cockerell, Director of the Museum between 1908 and 1937. He

ENGLISH BOW PORCELAIN

is said to have remarked, 'I found it a pig stye, I turned it into a palace'. The Early Italian Renaissance paintings are reached through the French Impressionist room to the left of the main stairs. Of late 15th-century date is a fine cassone panel, from a marriage chest, appropriately decorated by Jacopo del Sellaio with part of the Story of Cupid and Psyche, composed almost in cartoon-strip style; across the room is a painting of the *Virgin with Saints* by Cosimo Rosselli. On a small wall nearby the delightful Florentine perspective setting of Domenico Veneziano's *Annunciation* can be seen.

Treasures of the later Italian Renaissance in the room beyond include the landscape of *Castel Gandolfo* by Claude Lorraine; the minute, mysterious Elsheimer of *Minerva and Venus*, painted on copper; Titian's *Rape of Lucretia* and *Venus and a Lute-player*; and Veronese's *Hermes, Herse, and Aglauros*. At the far end of this large Italian room, past Canaletto's works, is the Flemish room with Joos van Cleve's good-humoured *Virgin and Child*, sketches by Rubens, early Flemish landscapes, and Spanish paintings by Murillo and others. Back through the large room an often unfairly ignored collection of Dutch 17th-century flower paintings is reached. The Dutch paintings room beyond has almost a history of Dutch landscapes from Van Goyen's low viewpoint to Philips de Koninck's panorama, and good small genre scenes by Jan Steen and Gerard Dou, a pupil of Rembrandt.

Through a small lecture theatre, and the Adeane gallery which houses temporary exhibitions, is the 20th-century gallery, containing works ranging from Graham Sutherland's *Crucifixion* to Kitaj's *Thanksgiving*.

Returning to the top of the main stairs the French Impressionist gallery is reached. This contains Renoir's *Gust of Wind*, Monet's *Le Printemps*, Pissarro's *Garden at Pontoise*, and Degas' moving *Au Café*. In the next room French paintings of the 17th to 19th centuries can be seen: from Poussin's *Rebecca and Eliezer at the Well*, a recent acquisition, to Fabre's *Allen Smith Contemplating the Arno*, and Courbet's fresh green *La Ronde Enfantine*.

To the right in the large room of 16th- to 18th-century paintings are excellent portraits by Van Dyck, Hogarth, Gainsborough, Reynolds and Raeburn, as well as Stubbs' *Gimcrack*, a recent

purchase. The 19th-century English room beyond contains Constable's *Hampstead Heath*, and Millais' startling gold and blue *Bridesmaid*. The next room is the early 20th-century paintings gallery with works by Sickert, Gilman and Gore influenced by Impressionism, and French works ranging from the sober structures of Cubism to the fresh colour of Matisse.

Folk Museum

Castle Street

The museum, opened in 1936, is housed in the former White Horse Inn—a 16th-century timber-framed building which has been altered and extended over the years. Its interior, with narrow stairs and well-worn creaky wooden floors is singularly appropriate as a setting for the numerous bygones collected over the last three centuries from Cambridge and the surrounding area.

The exhibits are fascinating and wide-ranging, and those relating to children and their toys are especially popular.

Other items of particular interest are arranged as follows, starting with tools and implements of local trades in the first ground-floor room. In the second room the inn's original bar, cooking and lighting equipment can be seen; there are also cigarette boxes, tea caddies, jelly moulds and sugar-loaf cutters. The third room has cooking and washing equipment, an amazing early refrigerator and vacuum cleaners. Upstairs samplers and similar handicrafts decorate one room, whilst the next has a wonderful variety of objects ranging from Aldermen's gowns to inn signs, and from a broadsheet of the execution of two murderers to a drawing of an 1877 local aerial machine which actually flew! Then come the children's rooms. The third floor contains a collection of fenlanders' tools.

Girton College

Huntingdon Road

Girton, the first women's college in either Oxford or Cambridge, originated in the movement to gain higher education for women. In 1869 Emily Davies, together with friends, rented Benslow House in Hitchin, 26 miles from Cambridge, and persuaded a few Cambridge lecturers to travel to Hitchin to teach the five women students. Hitchin had been chosen because it kept the female students well away from the male undergraduates, but when the Benslow House lease ended in 1872 it was decided to move nearer to Cambridge, and Girton, 2½ miles from the town centre, was chosen—still a safe distance from temptation.

The initial college had only one wing and a small hall, but as the number of students grew other buildings by Alfred Waterhouse and his son were added. Its remoteness has compensations; no other college has so much open space and garden around it—nearly 50 acres in all.

By 1881 women were allowed to attend University lectures and take examinations, but it was not until 1948—after much hostility—that the first woman graduate at Cambridge was awarded a degree.

As well as being the first Oxbridge women's college, Girton can also claim other firsts. It was the first college to have rooms opening off corridors not off separate staircases, and the first women's college to admit men.

Gonville and Caius College

Trinity Street and Senate House Passage

The college's name commemorates its two founders. The first of these, Edmund Gonville, was responsible for the hall which was built around Gonville Court after 1353. Behind the 18th-century ashlar façades of this court many of the 14th- and 15th-century buildings still exist. John Keys, latinised to Caius (but still pronounced Keys), re-founded the college in 1557 and became Master in 1559. He built Caius Court with its south side open, 'lest the air from being confined within a narrow space should become foul, and so do harm to us, and still more to Gonville's College'. Caius was also responsible for one of the jewels of the college, the Gate of Honour, which links Caius Court and

GONVILLE AND CAIUS
GATE OF HONOUR

Senate House Passage. This is the third of Dr Caius' gates which are remarkable for their early (1565–75) use of classical details. The new student entered through the Gate of Humility, now rebuilt in the Master's garden, passed through Virtue (still the entrance to Caius Court) to his lodging, and out through Honour to his graduation.

The chapel, between Gonville and Caius Courts, dates originally from the 14th century though it has been altered and extended over the years. It contains three remarkable tombs high up on its walls, those of Thomas Legge—Master of the college in the early 17th century, of Stephen Perse—founder of the Perse School, and of Dr Caius.

From Trinity Street and King's Parade the most obvious part of Caius (the abbreviated name by which the college is usually known) is Alfred Waterhouse's 19th-century building around Tree Court.

Caius College has always had strong links with the medical sciences, Caius himself being a Norfolk physician who had studied at Europe's leading medical school of the time, Padua, as well as at Gonville Hall. In his will Dr Caius provided for the cleaning of pavements and gutters inside and outside the college. A little later, at the end of the 16th century, William Harvey, who discovered the circulation of blood, graduated from the college.

Great St Andrew's Church

St Andrew's Street

Great St Andrew's, or St Andrew the Great Church, is no longer used as a place of worship, but its eye-catching position opposite Christ's College has made its future a centre of controversy. In 1842 the church was completely rebuilt, by subscription, in late 15th-century Gothic style. Because it contains many memorials, including one to Captain James Cook, the current proposal to turn it into shops is bitterly opposed.

Great St Mary's Church

King's Parade

St Mary the Great Church, known after 1352 as Great St Mary's, and commonly called the University Church, used to be the administrative and ceremonial centre of the University, and distances from Cambridge are measured from here. It has undergone two major rebuildings: the first followed a fire in 1290 (parts of the chancel walls are all that remain of this); the second began in 1478, most of the building being completed by 1514. The tower, however, was not finished until nearly 100 years later when Robert Grumbold added the corner turrets. It is well worth climbing the tower for the view of the city it provides.

St Mary's Late Perpendicular style of building is seen at its best from the inside. The roof, the original timbers for which were given by Henry VII, was repaired and preserved by the elder James Essex in 1726. As the University Church, Great St Mary's has hosted many famous preachers and pressure for more seating accommodation led to the building of the galleries in the 18th century.

An unusual feature of the church is the pulpit which runs on brass rails and can be moved from one side of the chancel to the other.

Guildhall

Market Hill

This building, on the south side of the Market Square, is where the locally elected council which governs the city is based. The present Guildhall was built in 1938–9 and contains two halls used for public functions, the Council Chamber, and working offices. Incorporated into the back of the building, facing Wheeler Street, are parts of the older Guildhall built between 1859 and 1895, and now housing the Tourist Information Centre.

Hobson's Conduit

Junction of Lensfield Road and Trumpington Road

This fountain, resembling a pepper-pot topped by a fir-cone, was erected in the Market Square in 1614 and moved to its present position in 1856. Water was brought in from Shelford, south of Cambridge, and distributed at the conduit-head; open gutters which used to flow with this water can still be seen in some streets such as Trumpington Street.

The conduit was named after Thomas Hobson (1544–1630), the Cambridge carrier who was its chief benefactor. This is the same Hobson who has become immortalised in the phrase 'Hobson's Choice', based on his practice of insisting that hirers took the horse nearest the door. This enforced rotation of horses prevented everyone choosing, and thus overworking, his best animals.

Holy Sepulchre Church

See Round Church

Holy Trinity Church

Market Street

Holy Trinity Church, on the corner of Market and Sidney Streets, is notable for its associations with the evangelical revival. Charles Simeon, Fellow of King's College and evangelical divine, became vicar in the 1780s; his style of preaching was carried on after his death in 1836. Simeon's memorial tablet is in the chancel and there is a bust in the entrance to the Old Schools, behind the Senate House. In the chancel there is also a memorial to the Reverend Henry Martyn who translated the New Testament into Hindustani and Persian. It is thought that Simeon's influence led to his decision to sail for India in 1805 to work as a missionary.

The church itself dates mainly from the 14th and 15th centuries, but has a 19th-century chancel. The 15th-century wooden roofs of the nave and transepts spring from stone corbels with angels.

Jesus College

Jesus Lane

A number of the buildings of Jesus College are adorned with three cock heads, the rebus or sign of Bishop John Alcock of Ely who in 1496 adapted the buildings of a suppressed nunnery, St Radegund's, for his new college. The high-walled passage-way 'The Chimney' leads from the 18th-century gateway by Robert Grumbold on Jesus Lane through the Tudor gatehouse into First or Outer Court. This, together with Cloister Court, contains the oldest buildings of the college.

The central archway in the 13th-century range on the east of Outer Court leads into Cloister Court, round which the layout and fabric of the Benedictine nunnery largely survive. Facing you as you enter Cloister Court are the fine Early English arches of the entrance to the former Chapter House. The Refectory, now the College Hall, was in the northern range, and on the south was the church. Much of the nave became the Master's Lodge, but the rest, with the crossing, the transepts and the chancel, is now the College Chapel, which is both a Gothic and a Gothic Revival monument. The chapel underwent two main periods of restoration in the 19th century. Pugin's glass and woodwork have transformed the chancel; Ford Madox Brown and Burne-Jones glass fills the nave and transept windows and the design of the crossing and nave roofs is by William Morris.

Jesus College has had several famous archbishops as members, the best known being Cranmer who compiled the English prayer book before his death as a martyr in Oxford (see page 30). Laurence Sterne, author of *Tristram Shandy*, and Samuel Taylor Coleridge (see page 32) were students at the college as, recently, was Prince Edward.

Kettle's Yard

Northampton Street

On the northern side of Northampton Street there appears to be a village green with an old people's home, a group of cottages with a simple modern barn-like building, and St Peter's church tower in the background. But the cottages, linked together by the barn-like extension gallery, house the art collection of Jim Ede, a personal exploration of 20th-century art. Jim Ede created the external setting as well as the interior, and left his extraordinary collection, which includes works by Henri Gaudier-Brzeska, Alfred Wallis and Ben Nicholson, to the University. The interiors are a surprisingly effective combination of domestic scale with a multi-level exhibition gallery. A separate gallery for visiting exhibitions has been added at the back, thereby extending the display space available.

King's College

King's Parade

King's College was founded in 1441 by Henry VI as a college for the scholars from his school at Eton. His first plans were for a small college of approximately 12 scholars, but then his ideas became grander with a scheme for a college of nearly 100 people, including 70 scholars and 16 choir boys. Sites were acquired and buildings demolished to make room for this new college, but only the Old Court (later rebuilt and now part of the Old Schools) and the chapel (see page 28) were built. Henry VI's connections with the college are commemorated by a statue which surmounts the fountain in Front Court.

The other college buildings, which date from the 18th century or later, were mostly built to be stylistically in keeping with the chapel. It pinnacles and windows are echoed in William Wilkins' screen wall and gatehouse on King's Parade. This and the south range of Front Court, containing the hall with its two wooden lanterns and splendid interior, is Gothic Revival of 1824–8.

Wilkins' south range continued westwards beyond Front Court, and has uninspired 19th- and 20th-century additions towards the river, and behind in Bodley's, Webb's and Chetwynd Courts.

In sharp contrast to the rest of King's is Gibbs' Fellows' Building which faces the King's Parade entrance. James Gibbs, architect of the Senate House, created this impressive west range between 1724 and 1732. Anywhere else but alongside the chapel, its monumental scale and splendid proportions would make it noteworthy.

Probably the most famous of King's 20th-century students was Lord Keynes, who improved the college's finances.

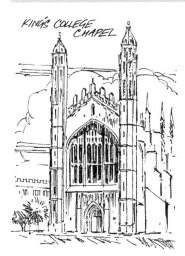

KING'S COLLEGE CHAPEL

King's Parade

Looking across the road from King's College one sees buildings with an appealing irregularity of height and style, shops below, living accommodation above. Between St Mary's and St Edward's Passages are 16th- and 17th-century buildings and a rare five-storey house of 1787. The rest of the Parade dates from the 18th and 19th centuries. Until the early 19th century the western side of King's Parade would have looked similar, with shops and houses reaching back as far as the screen wall of King's College which replaced them in the 1820s.

Leys School, The

Trumpington Road

Situated on a visually prominent site on the corner of Trumpington Road and Fen Causeway, this public school was established in the mid-1870s, as a Methodist foundation. Although it was originally open only to boys, it is now co-educational. Today's school shows a great mixture of buildings, the oldest of which, as shown on Baker's 1830 map, is the headmaster's house; other buildings are very new. The gateway and library, opened by George V in 1914, were designed by the architect Sir Aston Webb.

Lion Yard

See Petty Cury

Little St Mary's Church

Trumpington Street

Originally dedicated to St Peter, the church gave its name to Peterhouse and served as the college chapel until 1632; church and college are joined by a gallery. When the church was rebuilt in the mid 14th century it was dedicated to St Mary, and although the church's proper name is St Mary the Less it is more commonly known as Little St Mary's. The church is aisleless and there is no division between nave and chancel. A memorial tablet to Godfrey Washington, who died in 1729, carries the arms of the Washington family, stars and stripes surmounted by an eagle, which is thought to be the basis for the United States' flag.

Magdalene College

Magdalene Street

Magdalene's First Court was built in the 15th and early 16th centuries for monks from the Benedictine monasteries of Crowland, Ely, Ramsey and Walden—modern replicas of whose coats of arms adorn its walls. At this time the college was known as Buckingham College, because of the patronage of the dukes of Buckingham. With the Dissolution of the Monasteries the college lost its money as well as its monks, but a few years later (in 1542) it was refounded by Sir Thomas Audley (of Audley End) who renamed it Magdalene College.

Second Court, reached through the screens passage, contains the late 17th-century Pepys Building which houses Samuel Pepys' library, his bookshelves, books and diary. The hall of 1519 divides the two courts; it was re-panelled during Queen Anne's reign and her coat of arms is above the High Table. The hall has portraits of Samuel Pepys and Charles Kingsley, and the portrait of another graduate—Marshal of the RAF Lord Tedder—faces that of an Honorary Fellow—T S Eliot—by the double staircase which leads to the gallery.

Across Magdalene Street there have been 20th-century adaptations of houses and the upper floors of shops to student accommodation. Also on this side of the road are Mallory Court (built in 1925–6 and altered in 1952–6), commemorating the Everest climber, and Sir Edwin Lutyen's Benson Court.

Mount Pleasant and Pound Hill

Anyone interested in urban renewal would find a walk in this area rewarding. In the 1950s Pound Hill was described as 'a humble residential district'; the description continues '. . . the whole area has a down-at-heel aspect though, in its variety, not without quaint and picturesque vistas'. By the 1970s it was derelict, but in the 1980s it has been intelligently revitalised, with its vistas renewed.

To appreciate the mixture of old and new buildings and the interplay of colour from the great variety of bricks, the following route can be taken. From Northampton Street walk up Pound Hill, along Haymarket Road, and uphill round Mount Pleasant, passing en route Edward's House and Storey's House built in contrasting dark red bricks. At the top of Mount Pleasant and downhill, in Shelly Row, are Storey's Almshouses in yellow brick. Covering the area between Shelly Row and Castle Street a group of modern, pinkish yellow flats are ranged round an open courtyard with a pleasing arrangement of outside staircases and enclosed balconies.

At the bottom of Shelly Row turn left through Castle Row and left up Castle Street. The brick and timber-framed cottages facing the Shire Hall, some plaster covered, now restored and re-opened as restaurants and shops, are the oldest buildings in the area. Turn round and continue down Castle Street to the Folk Museum.

There are also blocks of modern buildings in the area and the successful restoration and adaptation of a medley of pleasant 19th-century buildings in Pound Hill and Haymarket Road is marred only by the 1884 Mission Hall and an aggressively ugly pub.

Museum of Archaeology and Anthropology

Downing Street

This beautifully arranged museum at the Tennis Court Road corner of the Downing Street site has coloured carpets on the ground floor which guide you round numbered, attractive display cases, through the early history of the world and Britain. The subjects covered, and some of the highlights, are as follows. Brown: the evolution of man, and his use of tools and plants. Fawn: European farmers and craftsmen. Blue (the largest section): Britain from 4000BC to the Middle Ages, emphasising Cambridgeshire, with exhibits including Iron Age scythes and napping shears, a firedog from Barton, varied Roman artefacts, and charming medieval alabaster figurines. Light brown: technology, including a reconstruction of the Somerset Sweet Track—an ancient constructed trackway. Red: Africa and Asia. Green: the Americas, with enchanting little statues of animals and humans displayed next door to black and white zigzag-patterned Pueblo pots.

Museum of Classical Archaeology

Sidgwick Avenue

A splendidly lit, long exhibition gallery, on the first floor of the new Department of Classics, houses a remarkable collection of over 500 plaster casts of Greek and Roman reliefs and sculptures, some coloured, some bronze. They are mostly life-size or larger and are displayed for study with every cast being clearly labelled. Just a few of the casts that may be seen are early Kores, the Delphi charioteer and the Venus de Milo. A cheap guide book lists them all.

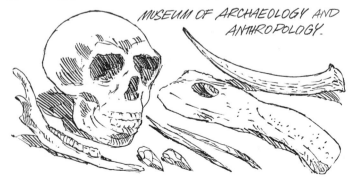

MUSEUM OF ARCHAEOLOGY AND ANTHROPOLOGY.

Museum of Technology

Riverside (off Newmarket Road)

When the Cheddar's Lane pumping station closed in 1968, after 73 years, enthusiasts saved the building and the steam engines from destruction and, against the odds, a museum unlike anything else in Cambridge was born. Its core is a collection of working engines including two 80 horsepower Hathorn-Davey engines with two Babcock and Wilcox water-tube boilers from 1894, and two 94 horsepower gas engines, driving centrifugal pumps, which date from 1909.

Other early machines have been added since the museum was founded, including radio, telex and computers. There is also a separate print shop with hand presses and machines for binding, cutting, and pressing books.

Museum of Zoology

Downing Street

Housed in a modern building, the museum is reached through the arch opposite the end of Tennis Court Road. Corals and shells are displayed on the top floor, with a wall-case of exotic birds on a half-way landing, and below a populated seabird landscape and another wall-case of birds. Skeletons fill the basement floor, where the exhibits are arranged to show the development of species. A wide range of animal life is covered, making it possible to compare the relative sizes of land and sea animals and of extinct and surviving species. There is also a room devoted to displays concerning man's ancestry.

New Hall

Huntingdon Road

In 1954 the third women's college, New Hall, was founded. It was initially based at the Hermitage in Silver Street, but 10 years later the college moved into its new white building in the north of the city. Several architectural features distinguish New Hall from other Cambridge colleges: the spine of the building is a tunnel, open on one side to a water garden below, which leads to the porter's lodge. The most visually striking part of the college is the domed dining hall with its petal-like segments.

Newnham College

Sidgwick Avenue

Two years after the foundation of Girton, Cambridge's second college for women, Newnham, came into being. Henry Sidgwick, Fellow of Trinity College, and Miss Clough, who became Principal, opened its first building in 1871, and the college moved to its present site in 1875. Six halls, joined by corridors, were built between 1875 and 1910, all designed by Basil Champneys in a red-brick Dutch style. They face an attractive open garden.

Other buildings have been added since, the most notable being the Principal's Lodge, designed by Louis Osmond. Its plan resembles a classical villa with a central court; the sheets of patterned plate glass, running from floor to roof, were designed by Geoffrey Clarke, who also worked on Coventry Cathedral.

Observatory, The

Madingley Road

To the west of Churchill College and well back on the north side of Madingley Road are the two domes of the University Observatory—a Doric-style building designed by John Clement Mead in 1822. The original dome in the centre is flanked by two projecting wings which contained houses for the Observer and the Deputy Observer. In 1838 the Northumberland Dome to the south-west was built at the expense of the 3rd Duke of Northumberland. The recently announced closure of the Royal Greenwich Observatory at Herstmonceux, East Sussex, and the amalgamation of its activities with those of the Cambridge Observatory will have important consequences for the study of astronomy.

Old Schools, The

Trinity Lane and Senate House Passage

University as opposed to college buildings came relatively late to Cambridge. However, in the confused cluster of the Old Schools, swallowed up and disguised by later work, a 14th-century building still survives. The Old Schools has two early, enclosed courts, concealed on the northern, Senate House Passage side by C R Cockerell's Library of 1837–42. This was built to house the University Library which moved out in 1934 to make room for the Squire Law Library.

Cobble (or Pebble) Court, the eastern and older of the two courts, has on the library side the Divinity School with the old Senate House above, finished in 1400. The original east side, facing King's Parade across the Senate House lawn, was replaced between 1754 and 1758 with a classical building by Stephen Wright. Its open walk with rusticated arches and windows above makes a perfect partnership with the Senate House.

Today the ground-floor rooms of Cobble Court are used as lecture rooms for the Law Faculty, the fine upstairs rooms as meeting rooms for the University's governing bodies and for receptions. What was the Senate House is now the Combination Room with an original timber roof and plasterwork, and William Morris' famous carpet from the house 'Clouds', on the floor.

In 1829 the Old Court of King's College was bought by the University and incorporated into the Old Schools. These buildings now house the University's administration offices. This Old Court of

King's College was begun in 1441, before the chapel. It was almost completely rebuilt in the 1860s, and in 1890 the unfinished gatehouse in Trinity Lane was, fortunately, restored and completed.

Our Lady and the English Martyrs Roman Catholic Church

Hills Road

In a commanding position at the corner of Lensfield Road and Hills Road, and with the highest spire in Cambridge, this church is one of the landmarks of the city. It was completed in 1890 in Gothic Revival style. The land was provided by the Duke of Norfolk, and Mrs Lyne-Stephens, wife of an art collector, paid for the building and endowed £5,000. Some of the features for which the church is known and remembered are its bells, the polygonal east end, and the richly carved stonework.

Pembroke College

Trumpington Street

The gateway, the only 14th-century college entrance remaining in place, and the range which continues round the corner into Pembroke Street are all that is left of the Countess of Pembroke's 1340s foundation. As you enter Old Court through the gateway the original chapel, now the Old Library with a fine plaster ceiling and bookcases of the 1690s, is on the left. On the right is the present chapel, built in the early 1660s by Sir Christopher Wren for his uncle, Matthew Wren, Bishop of Ely. It was Wren's first finished building and contains rare cushions of Turkey work, a type of knotted eastern carpet. Ahead is the College Hall, an 1875 replacement by Alfred Waterhouse, and the screens passage between the hall and kitchen leads into Ivy Court—built in the 17th century. The simple regularity of the north range, each dormer window with a pediment directly over two rectangular windows, contrasts with the more complex style of the later south range, the Hitcham Building.

Past members of the college include Nicholas Ridley, the Protestant martyr, Edmund Spenser, author of *The Faerie Queen*, and William Pitt the Younger, the 18th-century politician and Prime Minister (see page 31).

PEMBROKE COLLEGE

Perse School

Hills Road

Founded in 1615 by Stephen Perse of Caius College, this school has moved twice: from Free School Lane to Hills Road (on the corner of Harvey Road), in 1890, and to its present, specially designed modern building in the centre of ample playing fields in 1960. It has been, in succession, grammar, direct grant, and independent school. A separate girls' Perse School, now in Panton Street, was opened in the late 19th century.

THE HALL, PETERHOUSE COLLEGE

Peterhouse

Trumpington Street

Cambridge's oldest college was founded by Hugh de Balsham, Bishop of Ely in the 1280s. The Hall on the south side of Old Court was begun in 1286, but was heavily reconstructed in the 1860s, as was the neighbouring Combination Room. This was Gothic Revival work: Sir George Gilbert Scott was the architect of the Hall, and William Morris and other members of his firm were responsible for the interiors of both this and the Combination Room. The rest of Old Court is of 15th-century origin with mid 18th-century re-facing. A gallery still joins the college to the neighbouring Little St Mary's Church which the college originally used as its chapel.

First Court was laid out between 1590 and the 1630s; its notable feature is the chapel, the central building which points towards the street. It was built in the late 1620s, when Matthew Wren was Master, by George Thompson to the design of an unknown architect. The east and west fronts of the chapel provide fascinating examples of the different ways in which classical and Gothic elements could be harmoniously combined.

Petty Cury/Lion Yard

In the past Petty Cury (or Kitchen), also known at one time as Cook's Row, was an area of cobbled alleyways, coaching inns, courtyards and stables extensively used by traders, travellers, students and locals alike. Conditions were crowded, and the yard of one of the inns, the Falcon, soon deteriorated into a slum of 300 people living with little sanitation. As people left the town-centre dwellings in favour of the suburbs, the inns closed and shops took their place.

In the 1960s and 1970s there was extensive redevelopment of the south side of Petty Cury, and the Lion Yard shopping precinct, named after the largest of the coaching inns on the site, was built. A focal point of the uninspiring pedestrian precinct is the large red lion outside the Public Library—this was used as the model for the lion which stands outside Waterloo Station in London. The Public Library contains an extensive Cambridgeshire Collection of local history material and frequently has displays of old prints of the town and county.

Pitt (University Press) Building

Trumpington Street

Edward Blore was the architect of this last phase of an early 19th-century group of buildings stretching between Silver Street and Mill Lane. A fund collected for a London statue of William Pitt gave its surplus for the 1831–3 frontage, hence the name. The Pitt Building with its impressive Tudor–Gothic tower and façade which faces Botolph Lane was the home of the University Press until the late 1960s, and examples of the work done by the Press are displayed in the entrance hall. Recently the buildings on the site behind the Pitt frontage have housed peripatetic University departments.

THE ROUND CHURCH

Queens' College

Silver Street

This most charming Cambridge college was, not surprisingly, the first to limit its opening to visitors. The gateway in Queens' Lane, with coloured roof bosses, leads into a 15th-century court with a 1642 sundial on the north range. The Hall in the west range has interior decoration by Bodley and Morris and fireplace tiles by Morris and Ford Madox Brown, with portraits of Erasmus and Elizabeth Woodville—Edward IV's wife. She was one of the two foundresses; the other was Margaret of Anjou, Henry VI's wife. Erasmus of Rotterdam, the Renaissance scholar and theologian, occupied the turret in the south-west corner of this early court between 1511 and 1514.

Cloister Court, through the screens passage, features a unique combination of brick cloister arcades with a timber-framed gallery—the President's Lodge. The brickwork is late 15th-century, the gallery probably Elizabethan. Walnut Tree and Friars' Courts, north of the first court, have a remarkable wealth of later buildings, from a 17th-century range along Queens' Lane to Sir Basil Spence's Erasmus Building of 1959—60. This was almost the first Cambridge college building in 'modern' style and caused great controversy when it was built.

Robinson College

Grange Road

Cambridge's newest college and the first undergraduate college founded for both men and women, is named after its creator, the television and racing millionaire David Robinson.

The college, built between 1977 and 1980 of hand-made Dorset bricks over a concrete framework, is often described as having a fortress-like appearance. A ramp entrance leads into a brick street between two walls, a layout quite unlike any other college court. The chapel in the street 'wall' has a stained-glass window by John Piper and its doorway is an attractive example of the decorative use of brickwork.

Round Church

Bridge Street

The Round Church or Church of the Holy Sepulchre, on the corner of Bridge and Round Church Streets, is one of Cambridge's best-known tourist attractions. Land was granted to members of the fraternity of the Holy Sepulchre by the Abbot of Ramsey early in the 12th century, and the church with its circular nave was built. Fifteenth-century alterations included the addition of a polygonal belfry, but this was destroyed during the 1841 restoration undertaken by Anthony Salvin for the Cambridge Camden Society. The members of this Cambridge-based society were devoted to the 'correct' restoration of churches and were determined to reinstate the original features. Consequently, what remains now is a wholly Norman church, albeit heavily restored. Most of the rectangular eastern additions date from 1841–3, except for parts of the chancel and its roof which are of 15th-century origin.

St Andrew the Great Church

See Great St Andrew's Church

St Bene't's Church

Bene't Street

St Bene't's, the oldest church in Cambridge, was built well before the Norman Conquest and the original Saxon features can be seen in the 'long and short' stonework at the corners of the tower, in the pairs of round-headed windows in the top storey of the tower, and in the tower arch inside the church featuring two carved lions. Two aisles were added to the Saxon church in the 14th century, and were later widened.

In about 1500 Dr Cosyn, Master of Corpus Christi College (formerly Bene't's College), joined the college and church by building a gallery which runs over the gateway in Free School Lane. Bene't is an abbreviation of Benedict; the apostrophe in the church's name is to indicate this.

St Bene't's has connections with several well-known Cambridge citizens. It was the burial place of Thomas Hobson the 17th-century carrier, and the church also has a Bible presented by him. Later in the 17th century the clerk of St Bene't's, a man named Fabian Stedman, invented the system of change-ringing, still used by bell-ringers today.

ST BENE'TS CHURCH

St Botolph's Church

Trumpington Street

The dedication of this church to the fenland saint of travellers, Botolph, suggests evidence of an early church, but the oldest surviving parts, the nave and aisles, only go back to the 14th century. The church was built near Trumpington Gate, where the road from London entered the medieval town, and travellers prayed here for a safe journey and also gave thanks when they returned safely home.

St Botolph's Church has some interesting features, especially an eye-catching Laudian font and cover. An octagonal structure in the churchyard is probably a well covering. The churchyard also contains memorials to two people responsible for much rebuilding and restoration in Cambridge: the tomb of James Essex and a memorial tablet to the mason Robert Grumbold who died in 1720.

St Catharine's College

Trumpington Street

An old college with later buildings and an almost melodramatic late 19th-century history (when there were public disputes over the election of a new Master), St Catharine's today presents an

attractive face to Trumpington Street. Founded in 1473 for the study of theology and philosophy, its three-sided Principal Court was the work of Robert Grumbold, Sir Christopher Wren's mason. The college has since expanded on each side, incorporating the former Bull Hotel which had been left to St Catharine's in 1626. Beyond the Bull site the college developed the area along King's Lane jointly with King's College and, across the river, opened St Chad's Hostel in 1981. Here the accommodation consists of shared flatlets.

St Edward's Church

St Edward's Passage

This church probably has Saxon origins, for it is dedicated to Edward the Confessor, the Saxon king. It has been much restored over the years, and the oldest remaining sections are the 13th-century tower and the chancel arch from around 1400. The two chapels on either side of the chancel were built for the members of Clare and Trinity Hall in the mid 15th century when their own church of St John Zachary was demolished to make way for King's College.

Reformation sermons were preached by Bilney, Barnes and Latimer from the early 16th-century pulpit still to be seen in the church.

St Giles' Church

Castle Street/Chesterton Lane

Although the present church dates from the 19th century, it was rebuilt on the site of a Norman church. Built in an Early English style, the church incorporates the chancel arch from its predecessor. Despite the joining together of several parishes, the church became redundant, and is now used as a Brass Rubbing Centre.

St John's College

St John's Street

Neighbour to Trinity College and its rival in size and wealth, St John's is some 35 years older and more compact, though it extends over both sides of the river. Some of Cambridge's finest architecture, spanning many periods from the early 16th century to the 1960s, can be found in its nine courts.

St John's, like Christ's, was founded by Henry VII's mother, Lady Margaret Beaufort, and her coat of arms decorate the splendid early 16th-century gatehouse with its original oak doors. To this day the college boat club is called Lady Margaret, as is Cambridge's first professorship of divinity. Lady Margaret died in 1509, but Bishop John Fisher, her Confessor, carried out her intentions for the building of the college. First Court was built between 1511 and 1516, Second Court between 1598 and 1602, and their skyline reveals the changes in style. Outstanding is the gatehouse leading from Second to Third Court, the Shrewsbury Tower, so-called because Mary, Countess of Shrewsbury, partly paid for Second Court.

A real architectural contrast is revealed in Third Court: the library on the north side was built in a hybrid Tudor–Gothic style in the 1620s, the other two sides in a classical idiom around 1670.

Over the river, and behind the 19th-century New Court, are the two courts of the 1963–7 Cripps Building, quite the most outstanding of the three buildings with which the Cripps Foundation of Nottingham has endowed Cambridge. Powell and Moya, the architects, designed a zigzag which relates sympathetically to the river and to Bin Brook, encloses a court behind New Court, and incorporates—a stroke of genius—two outstanding old buildings into a second court. The Norman 'School of Pythagoras', a house not a school, adjoins the gabled 17th-century Merton Hall.

St Mary the Great Church

See Great St Mary's Church

St Mary the Less Church

See Little St Mary's Church

St Mary Magdalene Chapel

See Stourbridge Chapel

St Michael's Church

Trinity Street

This 14th-century Decorated Gothic building opposite Caius College retains its original quality in spite of restoration by Sir George Gilbert Scott in 1849 after a fire destroyed the roof. It was built in 1326 on the site of an earlier church, and served both as parish church and as the chapel of Michaelhouse, a college of 1324 now incorporated in Trinity College. In 1966 the nave, which contains a full-length portrait of Charles I, became Great St Mary's parish hall. Worship continues in the larger chancel with 15th-century painted stalls, now St Michael's Chapel, and in Hervey de Stanton's south chapel with its ogee arched niches on either side of the east window.

St Peter's Church

Castle Street

This tiny church, at less than 35ft long one of the smallest in the country, has a Norman font on which Tritons are carved—variously described as 'unusual decoration' or 'grotesque sculpture', depending on your taste. The church is of Norman foundation, with a 14th-century tower, but by the middle of the 18th century the building was no longer used for worship and stood roofless and windowless. It was rebuilt, on a reduced scale, in 1781, using materials from the old church. However, in the 20th century it once again is no longer in use and is in the hands of the Redundant Churches Fund.

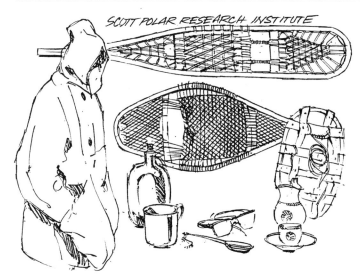

SCOTT POLAR RESEARCH INSTITUTE

Scott Polar Research Institute (SPRI)

Lensfield Road

The Institute, an international centre for polar studies, was founded in memory of the explorer, Captain Robert Falcon Scott in 1920 and moved to its present building in 1934. The public museum, with its domed ceiling displaying maps of the Arctic and Antarctic, has fascinating examples of the cumbersome equipment carried on British polar explorations in the 19th and 20th centuries. Other smaller exhibits include arts and crafts of the polar regions, such as scrimshaw and Eskimo sculpture, and there are displays illustrating the wildlife of the region and modern scientific research.

The Institute also has other collections not on public display, as well as a library containing the world's largest single collection of material on the polar regions, including hundreds of water-colours and thousands of photographs.

Sedgwick Museum of Geology

Downing Street

Since 1904 this building, situated in the Downing Place corner of the Downing Street site, has housed the collection of fossils begun by Adam Sedgwick, Woodwardian Professor of Geology at Cambridge from 1818 to 1873. Clearly marked cases are arranged in order of geological time with appropriate fossils and casts. Special exhibits include a

display on the evolution of the elephant family, and a reconstructed iguanodon skeleton. There are also skeletons of an Irish elk (bought for £140 in 1835) and of a hippopotamus from Barrington, near Cambridge, the latter providing a vivid reminder that the British climate has often changed over geological time.

At the far end of the displays is the Museum Woodwardian, claimed to be the oldest intact geological collection in the world, made by Dr John Woodward (1665–1728) and stored in its original walnut cabinets. Facing this is a fascinating display of Sedgwick's life and his contribution to geology.

Outside the museum, on Downing Street, prehistoric animals carved in the stonework of the building can be seen.

Selwyn College

Grange Road

Selwyn is a late 19th-century college, founded in memory of Bishop Selwyn of New Zealand and Lichfield with the aim of preserving Anglican values in the University. Before 1957 all Fellows, Scholars and Exhibitioners had to be Anglicans and Selwyn did not become a full member college of the University until this regulation was lifted. Sir Arthur Blomfield's Old Court with its outstanding chapel, closed by an early 20th-century hall range and with a garden to the east, has a comfortable warmth. This is lacking in the 1966–8 Cripps Court off Cranmer Road.

Senate House

King's Parade

James Gibbs' rectangular University 'parliament' building, lying alongside a grassy sward at the end of King's Parade, is certainly eye-catching. Built between 1722 and 1730, it successfully combines various classical styles—'a noble and complete entity' as one observer put it. The exterior suggests a building of considerable internal complexity, but the plan of the interior is actually quite simple—a hall with a small ante-chamber. The decoration, however, elaborate, particularly the gallery around three sides and the panelling of the dais. Some of the interior woodwork is by James Essex senior. It is here that degrees are conferred and University policy is debated and put to the vote.

The Senate House is fronted by a well-manicured lawn, at the centre of which stands a copy in bronze of the huge Warwick Vase. It stands on a stone plinth pedestal which was inscribed by Eric Gill in 1936. The railings separating the lawn from King's Parade date from 1730, and are some of the earliest cast-iron railings in the country.

Shire Hall

Castle Street

This uncompromising rectangular building of 1932, facing Castle Mound, had a top storey added after World War II. All that remains of earlier buildings on the site is the recently cleaned old Police Station on Castle Street. In 1986–7 makeshift buildings at the back were cleared and an area as far as Victoria Road covered with a colourful complex of new buildings for the County Council's use and for business premises. This development is an interesting example of collaboration between local government and private enterprise.

Sidgwick Site

Between Sidgwick Avenue and West Road

In 1954 the University decided to develop this area as a centre for the arts faculties. Buildings include Lady Mitchell Hall, built in 1963–4 to seat 450, and named after the wife of Sir Godfrey Mitchell, chairman of the contractors, Wimpey. The name of the late 19th-century economist Alfred Marshall was given to the prestigious economics library.

One architectural firm, that run by Sir Hugh Cassons, planned the site but other architects were responsible for particular buildings within the overall plan. The most notorious is the triangular History Faculty building at the north-west corner, completed in 1968. James Stirling, the architect, has received international acclaim and rewards for this building, but the roof leaked, the glass cascade down the front made the library below oppressively hot and some of the harsh red bricks and tiles covering the sides fell off and have had to be replaced. At one time the University seriously considered pulling it down.

Sidney Sussex College

Sidney Street

Sidney Sussex College is best known as Oliver Cromwell's college, and it possesses a contemporary portrait by Samuel Cooper and—more macabre—the Lord Protector's head, as a plaque in the ante-chapel records. The late 16th-century college, founded by Frances Sidney, Countess of Sussex, was transformed in 1831–2 by Sir Jeffrey Wyatville. He cement-rendered the Tudor–Gothic Hall Court and also Chapel Court where the chapel was rebuilt and the eastern range resurfaced. Although the façades of the two courts have now been modernised, the effect remains drab.

Two Civil War generals on opposite sides, George Goring the Royalist and the Parliamentarian Earl of Manchester, are amongst the past members of the college.

Stourbridge Chapel

Newmarket Road

Stourbridge Chapel, the Leper Chapel, or, more correctly, St Mary Magdalene Chapel, is a fine example of Norman architecture. Built in the early 12th century, it was once the chapel for the leper hospital at Barnwell, and later a store for the Stourbridge Fair. The University took over the building early in the 19th century and kept it in good repair, as has the Cambridge Preservation Society in whose care it has been since 1954.

Theatre Royal

See Festival Theatre

Trinity College

Trinity Street

Trinity is a royal college in several senses. It was founded by two kings, has housed royal undergraduates (Prince Charles was the most recent of these and his great-great-grandfather, later Edward VII, preceded him though he did not live in college), and the Master is not elected by the Fellows as in most colleges but appointed by the Crown. Recent incumbents have included G M Trevelyan, the historian and Macaulay's great-nephew, and R A Butler, the Conservative statesman.

Henry VIII created Trinity out of several pre-Reformation institutions, the main ones being King's Hall, Michaelhouse and Physwick Hostel. King's Hall had been founded about 200 years earlier by Edward III, but King's Hostel, a range extending north of Great Court, is all that remains of the 14th- to 15th-century college buildings. King Edward's Tower, built in 1428–32 as the gateway for King's Hall, and now the entrance to King's Hostel, became a model for later college gateways. Great Gate, the present entrance to Great Court, was also built for King's Hall, between 1490 and 1535. Since the early 17th century a statue of Henry VIII has stood in majesty over the gate, his majesty reduced, however, by the chair leg which replaces his sceptre. This was the result of a 20th-century student prank but is perhaps appropriate for the royal intruder in Edward III's place.

Trinity straggles over a large area from Sidney Street to Grange Road but the heart of the college consists of Great Court and Nevile's Court, both the creation of Dr Thomas Nevile, Master from 1593 to 1615. Great Court, Cambridge's largest enclosed court, owes its charm to its very lack of symmetry, resulting from the welding together of buildings of different elevations and periods with a central focus in Nevile's 1601–2 fountain. Many later piecemeal alterations have given some uniformity to the court. The film *Chariots of Fire* has made famous Trinity's undergraduate challenge—completing a run round the court while the clock strikes midnight. Trinity's chapel, on the north side of Great

Court, cannot compete with that of King's, but it is an interesting Counter-Reformation building in Gothic style begun in Mary I's reign, with an 18th-century screen and stalls. In the ante-chapel is Roubiliac's statue of Isaac Newton and statues of Francis Bacon, Macaulay and Tennyson. Great Court also contains the Judges' Suite in its north-west corner. This is where, in the past, judges arriving for the Assizes would be accommodated.

Beyond Great Court is Nevile's Court with one of Cambridge's major buildings on its western side. This is Sir Christopher Wren's Library of 1676–95, a striking contrast with the Elizabethan Hall opposite. The Library has two aspects, to Nevile's Court and to the river; the façades have a subtle external design which conceals the internal floor level. The Library not only contains a fine collection of books and manuscripts but also busts and statues of some of the college's famous students.

FOUNTAIN · TRINITY COLLEGE

Trinity Hall

Trinity Lane

Its compact situation between Trinity Lane and the river, and Clare College and Garret Hostel Lane gives Trinity Hall a friendly atmosphere. Founded in 1350 by William Bateman, Bishop of Norwich, it was originally known as 'The College of the Scholars of the Holy Trinity of Norwich'. Principal Court was built in the college's early days, but 18th-century ashlar now disguises it. The college chapel has a fine plaster ceiling and brasses. Fourteenth-century clunch and red brick can be seen in the north wall of Principal Court. From the west of North Court a staircase leads to an imaginative 20th-century range by Wyn Roberts and Geoffrey Clarke where a flower-decked terrace outside a bar and lecture room faces the gardens. Below is the Elizabethan library with its original desks, shelves and chained books.

Union Society, The

Bridge Street

Behind the Round Church is a multi-coloured brick building which has served as a political nursery for many of Britain's outstanding politicians. Built by Alfred Waterhouse in 1866, the club facilities, library and debating chamber—which is a miniature of the House of Commons save for its gallery—have provided a discussion forum for over 120 years. In 1866 the Society was already some 50 years old although it had been suppressed in 1817 because it discussed politics! However these have been the life-blood of debates ever since, together with forays into awkward cultural and social questions.

University Library, The

West Road

There has been a University Library in Cambridge for nearly 600 years. Since 1662 it has been entitled to receive free a copy of every book published in the United Kingdom and is now one of five copyright libraries in the country. For many centuries the library was housed in the Old Schools but, despite frequent additions to the space available, it still outgrew its accommodation. The present building with its 160ft-high tower, designed by Sir Giles Gilbert Scott, was opened in 1934 by George V, and in 1972 a large extension was added. With its strong vertical lines, the library's exterior is often said to resemble Stockholm Town Hall. The Reading Room, which is about 190ft long, houses only a minute fraction of the millions of books in the library.

Westminster College

Madingley Road

The red-brick college which closes the view at the northern end of Queen's Road is the grandest of five independent theological colleges. Opened in 1899 for a London Presbyterian college founded in 1844, in 1967 it absorbed Cheshunt, the oldest Cambridge theological college, which was situated in Bateman Street near the Botanic Garden.

Whipple Museum of the History of Science

Free School Lane

R S Whipple's collection began the museum in 1944 and in 1952 it moved into the old Perse School hall which was restored in 1976. Among much else the hall contains early surveying equipment (theodolite and chain), navigation instruments (astrolobes, quadrants and sextants), and a grand orrery—a clockwork model of the planetary system—dating from about 1750 flanked by two globes. In a second room microscopes, chemical balances and fascinating electrostatic generators can be seen.

Wolfson College

Barton Road

In 1965 University College, a graduate foundation, was set up by the University in Bredon House, Selwyn Gardens. However, a grant from the Wolfson Foundation in 1972 transformed the site, and the name was changed accordingly. The traditional layout, in courts, has been achieved by uniting the existing house with new ranges, some of stone, others of mixed shades of brick. Thin slabs of granite, from parts of the stonework of London Bridge, were used to floor the entrance hall.

AA

Pocket Guide
to
CAMBRIDGE

CITY WALKS • CITY WALKS

Around Castle Mound

This walk, in the northern part of the city, takes in many of the sites important in Cambridge's early history, as well as a 20th-century art gallery. It also includes a visit to Castle Mound, with its views over the whole city.

Allow 1 hour. Start at the Round Church and continue north-westwards along Bridge Street.

Round Church ①. Built in 1130, this is the oldest of only four surviving round churches in England. The style was introduced by the returning crusaders in remembrance of the Church of the Holy Sepulchre, place of pilgrimage in Jerusalem.

Bridge Street ②. Finely renovated buildings on the right of this street make it possible to re-create mentally the scene of medieval Cambridge. This was the main street, following the line of the earlier Roman road, leading to the Great Bridge. It

PORTUGAL PLACE

pawnbroker's symbol; not the commonplace sign it was many years ago.

Immediately before the church turn right into *Portugal Place*. **Portugal Place ③.** St Clement's Church, dating from the early 13th century, marks the entry to this peaceful residential quarter so close to the city centre. Much has changed here since medieval times, when thatched cottages housed boatmen and college servants. Many properties, however, are still owned by the colleges; nowadays they are used to accommodate students. The exclusion of vehicles (bar the odd bicycle) has long been enforced, as the police notice at the end of the street on the wall of number 10 Portugal Street bears out.

housed many more traders than today, and several inns and stables. The alley between the two pubs, the Mitre and the Baron of Beef, once led to a courtyard containing 11 houses and, 400 years ago, a brewery. Before the church, on your right, look above the door of the clothes shop to see the three balls of the

Continue into Portugal Street, turn left along Park Parade, then right to follow the riverside path on Jesus Green to the lock. Here cross the footbridge and turn left. At the traffic-lights at the end of Chesterton Lane turn right into Castle Street, past St Giles' Church on the corner. **St Giles' Church** ④. A church has stood here since Norman times, but nothing now remains of the original building although the chancel arch dates back to the Norman period. This is the oldest part of Cambridge, where the Romans first mounted guard over their river crossing at the foot of the hill. Long after the Romans departed, the higher ground on this side of the river made it a natural point for both defence and settlement.

Opposite the church stands the Cambridge and County Folk Museum. **Folk Museum** ⑤. Until 1934 this was the White Horse Inn, one of 11 pubs in the street during the last century. A wide chimney-breast, now blocked up, provided a hiding hole—popular no doubt with the highwaymen of earlier days. In keeping with its original use, the museum contains a Bar Parlour Room, along with other domestic reminders of the past.

Continue up the hill, past St Peter's Church on the left. **St Peter's Church** ⑥. A population decline in the parish has left this little church in the hands of the Redundant Churches Fund. Although built in the early 12th century, Roman bricks (looking like rough red tiles) can be seen built into the walls by the main door. Until 1802 a gaol existed close by, and many an escaping prisoner is said to have clung to the altar rails seeking sanctuary in this church.

Castle Mound lies further up Castle Street, in the

KETTLE'S YARD

grounds of Shire Hall. **Castle Mound** ⑦. Climb to the top for a view of the Cambridge skyline, contrasting the medieval spires of colleges with later buildings such as the University Library. The mound is all that is left of the Norman castle, built first in wood and then in stone. It was little used after the 15th century, and its walls were dismantled with the stone being used instead for some of the college buildings.

Turn left off Castle Street into Whymans Lane. A pub, The Three Tuns, once stood in front of Bell's Court and was a favourite haunt of highwayman Dick Turpin. Continue down Pound Hill and at the bottom bear left into Northampton Street to Kettle's Yard Gallery. **Kettle's Yard** ⑧. The area known as Kettle's Yard used to be occupied by a number of cottages where sanitation was poor and conditions cramped. However, by the 1930s most of these had been demolished, leaving only two of the larger buildings which were later converted into one. Here Jim Ede created the Gallery, as he wanted to provide a domestic environment in which to house works of art. The collection, open afternoons only, contains drawings and sculptures, with many works dating from the 1920s and 1930s.

At the traffic-lights, turn

right down Magdalene Street, passing Magdalene College on the left. **Magdalene College** ⑨. This was the last college to surrender its all-male status but will admit women after 1988. It is particularly famous for the library collection of Samuel Pepys, a former member of the college. The picturesque timber-framed buildings on the west side of the road are all owned by Magdalene too. Had the college not run out of money in 1930 they would have been demolished to make way for a grand new court, but fortunately they have survived, preserving another medieval reminder of old Cambridge.

Continue over the bridge. **The Bridge** ⑩. The river was first forded at this point by the Romans, so that their great road, *Via Devana*, could continue from Colchester to Chester. Saxons, Danes and Normans have all settled at this focal point, as Cambridge grew into an important inland port. Various bridges have, at times, spanned the river, the first believed to have been built before 875. Nowadays punts are the only river traffic to float gently under the bridge.

Continue along Magdalene Street and Bridge Street back to the Round Church.

Streets Ancient and Modern

From the very centre of the city, this walk follows the southern limit of the medieval town, passes three colleges, crosses Jesus Green and returns along one of the main shopping streets.

Allow 1½ hours. Start in the Market Square.

Market Square ①. The original market-place, an L-shaped area at the very heart of the medieval town, was smaller than the present one, trading mainly in corn, poultry, meat and butter. It has been the scene of many an event over the centuries, not least the Great Fire of 1849 which destroyed many of the surrounding buildings and resulted in today's open market-place. The fire raged through the night, and lines of men supplied buckets of water from as far away as the river. Now the market sells an enormous range of goods, but continues to be a colourful and thriving affair.

Facing the Guildhall, walk round the building to the right, and into Peas Hill. **Peas Hill ②.** This area may appear flat, but in early days it was much higher than the surrounding marshy ground. Peas Hill was, in the past, well known for its many fish stalls. Beneath this area is a vast network of cellars and tunnels covering a quarter of an acre, which have at times been used as wine vaults, and then as air-raid shelters during World War II.

Turn right into Bene't Street, then left before the church into Free School Lane. **St Bene't's Church ③.** The tower of the church dates back to Saxon times and is the oldest surviving building in the county. The church served as a chapel for Corpus Christi College, next door, and a gallery

MARKET SQUARE

connecting the two can still be seen from the lane.

Continue along Free School Lane, passing the Whipple Museum of the History of Science on the right. **Free School Lane ④.** During its long history the Free School Lane area has housed an Augustinian friary, the old Botanic Garden, lecture rooms and the famous Cavendish Laboratory, as well as the Perse School which probably gave the road its name. The Whipple Museum, situated in the old school hall, has many fine exhibits relating to the scientific background of this site.

At the end of the road turn left into Downing Street. This follows the line of the King's Ditch, marking the southern boundary of medieval Cambridge. On

reaching St Andrew's Street turn left; opposite is Emmanuel College. **Emmanuel College ⑤.** Like several of the other colleges, Emmanuel was built on the site of a former friary and some of the old buildings were adapted to college life. The present chapel was added a little later and was designed by Christopher Wren.

Continue northwards along St Andrew's Street to Christ's College and St Andrew the Great Church. **Christ's College and St Andrew the Great Church ⑥.** The King's Ditch, famous more for its unsanitary nature than defensive potential, followed a line from Downing Street along to Hobson Street. At this point the ditch crossed close to Barnwell Gate, one of the main entrances to the town. The church at this junction, known previously as St Andrew without Barnwell Gate, contains a memorial to Captain Cook, whose widow and two sons are buried here. Christ's College opposite, founded by Lady Margaret Beaufort, has many famous past students including John Milton and Charles Darwin. Originally known as God's House, the college has some 16th and 17th century (and earlier) buildings, but substantial reconstruction and re-facing took place in the 18th and 19th centuries.

Bear right along Hobson Street which turns right into King Street. **King Street ⑦.** This street has changed considerably over the years, especially on its northern side where the colleges have built new residences for students. Previously, it had the atmosphere of village life, with small shops, almshouses and many pubs, the last-mentioned resulting in the 'King Street Run', a University tradition to attempt to drink a glass of beer in each of the 13 or 14

pubs before closing time. Only five pubs now remain, the Champion of the Thames being the oldest.

At the roundabout, cross to Victoria Avenue, with Jesus College on the left and Midsummer Common on the right. **Midsummer Common** ⑧. Before enclosure, this was an area of open pasture, dissected by ditches and meandering tracks. A fair has been held on the common every midsummer since the 13th century and although the fair today has altered

considerably in character, it still attracts many people to its amusements and lively atmosphere.

Turn left along the path at the end of Jesus College onto Jesus Green, continue down Lower Park Street, left into Park Street, and at the junction with Jesus Lane turn right past the Pitt Club. **Pitt Club** ⑨. The classical frontage of this building may seem surprising when compared to its neighbours, until you consider it was built in the mid 19th century to house a mock

Roman Bath. However, the scheme did not last long as the premises were taken over by the political Pitt Club in 1866. The building's function has again diversified; part of it is now used as a restaurant.

Turn left into Sidney Street. **Sidney Street** ⑩. Sidney Street was one of the principal routes through the town, following the line of the Roman road towards the bridge over the Cam. Now it is a busy shopping street, retaining some of the outfitters and older stores that gave it an atmosphere of some elegance during the 19th century.

Just before the junction with Hobson Street turn right into Petty Cury. **Petty Cury/ Lion Yard** ⑪. The Lion Yard shopping complex on the left retains nothing of the architecture, alleyways or cobblestones that characterised the area until the mid 20th century. There used to be numerous coaching inns here too, and it was the largest of these, the Red Lion, which gave its name to the modern development.

Continue along Petty Cury to return to the Market Square.

Quiet Back Streets and the Upper River

A short walk, taking in four colleges, the splendid Fitzwilliam Museum, the upper river and some of the city's quieter—but just as fascinating—back streets.

Allow 1 hour. Start at the corner of Mill Lane and Trumpington Street where the University Press Building stands.

University Press (Pitt) Building ①. Printing was an early industry in Cambridge, starting in 1521. The first publications were mostly Bibles and prayer books, although works such as Newton's *Principia* appeared by the 18th century. This imposing church-like building of 1833 housed the University Press until recently, and still has a showroom and offices.

HOBSON'S CONDUIT

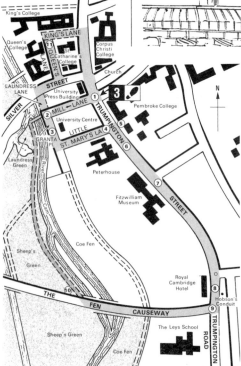

Walk down Mill Lane—passing University lecture halls and other departments—to the Mill Pond. **Mill Pond** ②. This tranquil spot was once a busy wharf area with barges bringing goods and grains to the mills which stood here. This was as far inland as boats could travel, thus establishing Cambridge as an important trading centre. Until the arrival of the railway in 1845 the river was a vital link for transporting goods.

Turn left at the bottom of Mill Lane passing the University Centre on the left. **University Centre** ③. The modern building overlooking the Mill Pond is used by graduates for recreational and social functions. Here a row of cottages once stood, whose tenants provided a laundry service for the University. Husbands and sons would collect washing from the colleges, wives and daughters would wash and iron. The open space over the river is known as Laundress Green, where lines of washing drying in the wind used to be a familiar sight.

Shortly turn left into Little St Mary's Lane, past a row of charming old houses to Little St Mary's Church. **Little St Mary's Church** ④. Built between 1340 and 1352, this church replaced an older one dedicated to St Peter. Peterhouse, next door, was the first college to be founded in Cambridge, and took its name from the church. Inside is a gallery connecting the two buildings, designed to prevent students 'losing' themselves between study and prayer. To the left of the entrance is a plaque in memory of the Reverend Godfrey Washington who belonged to the same family as the American, George Washington. The church-yard is one of the most peaceful in Cambridge.

Cross Trumpington Street to reach Pembroke College.
Wren Chapel ⑤. The chapel of Pembroke College is the first completed work of Sir Christopher Wren, built in 1663–4 in pure classical style. His uncle, the Bishop of Ely, was imprisoned in the Tower of London during the Civil War, and vowed—should he be released—to thank the Almighty in some way. To this end, he asked his nephew to design the college chapel.

On leaving Pembroke turn left down Trumpington Street towards Peterhouse.
Peterhouse ⑥. Peterhouse dates from the late 13th century. In the 18th century the poet Thomas Gray was a student at the college and the window from which he is reputed to have escaped down a rope-ladder into a tub of water put there by fellow students (see page 31) can be seen top left.

Further along Trumpington Street is the imposing building of the Fitzwilliam Museum.
Fitzwilliam Museum ⑦. This temple to the Arts was opened to the public in 1848. Richard, 7th Viscount Fitzwilliam, bequeathed to the University his library of 10,000 books, paintings and manuscripts. Income from investments was to provide a building to house the collection and to buy new works. The contents of the museum are now vast, and many items are housed in the modern extension which was constructed in keeping with the original design of the building.

The gutters running along both sides of the street were used to bring fresh water to the town. Continue to Hobson's Conduit at the corner of Lensfield Road.
Hobson's Conduit ⑧. The conduit used to stand in the Market Square where it marked the end of the artificial watercourse, built jointly by the town and University to bring fresh

PETERHOUSE COLLEGE CHAPEL.

PEMBROKE COLLEGE CHAPEL DETAIL

water from springs outside the town. In its original position the conduit was surrounded by railings to which, it has been recorded, offenders who had been sentenced to a public whipping were chained.

Just past the Royal Cambridge Hotel turn right down Fen Causeway. The Leys School stands to the left.
Leys School ⑨. Founded in the mid-1870s, this was the first public school to be set up by the Methodist Church—in order to rival those of the Church of England. The famous book *Goodbye Mr Chips* was written by a master of the Leys, who based his character on a colleague at the school. It remained an all-boys' institution until 1984, when girls were admitted to the sixth form.

Continue along the
Causeway, turn right just after the river bridge and walk along the footpath looking across to Coe Fen.
Coe Fen ⑩. This area of common fen land, so close to the city centre, gives an idea of how difficult it would have been to extend building during medieval times. The low-lying meadow land is still prone to flooding, but provides the unusual city sight of grazing cattle and wild flowers.

Follow the path back to the Mill Pond, cross the weir and turn left down Laundress Lane. Note the public notice on the wall dated 1857. Turn right into Silver Street, then left along Queens' Lane.
Queens' Lane ⑪. This quiet, narrow lane was once the southern end of 'Milne Street', the main street of early Cambridge which led down to the wharfs and King's Mill. Queens' College on the left has buildings dating back to 1448 including one of the few half-timbered structures in the colleges. St Catharine's College on the right was built facing onto this busy street, but changed its entrance to Trumpington Street when the lane declined in importance.

Turn right at the end of the lane, go through the passage-way to Trumpington Street, then turn right again back to the start of the walk.

Expansion to the West

As the University grew, the town centre became a crowded jumble of buildings. From the hustle and bustle of this busy area, the walk passes by the more recent buildings west of the river, returning via the Backs.

PUNTING ON THE BACKS

Allow ¾ hour. Start at the junction of King's Parade and Bene't Street and walk south along Trumpington Street.

Trumpington Street ①. Unlike other medieval colleges, Corpus Christi—on the left—was founded by townspeople rather than a monarch or famous person. As well as famed scholars, the college also has a ghost! One story tells of the Master's daughter hiding her student lover in a spring-loaded chest. He died of suffocation, she of a broken heart, and his spirit is said to haunt the Old Court. Opposite is St Catharine's College where in order to build the three-sided courtyard a row of 17th-century inns was demolished. One of these was owned by Thomas Hobson, who also hired out horses. He always insisted on the horse nearest the door being taken, hence the expression 'Hobson's

Choice'—or lack of!

Continue to St Botolph's Church at the end of Silver Street. **St Botolph's Church** ②. In medieval times this church lay close to the southern gates of the town, hence its dedication to St Botolph, the patron saint of travellers. In the attractive churchyard is a memorial to James Essex Junior, a notable 18th-century architect who designed buildings for many of the older colleges.

Turn right down Silver Street. **Silver Street Bridge** ③. Passing Queens' Lane, formerly a main street, on the right, we come to the river and a crossing point of some importance at a time when Cambridge thrived on its river trade. Long before the colleges were built, barges brought grain to the wharfs and mills that stood around the Mill Pond. The wooden bridge that now connects the old and new buildings of Queens' College (on the right) is the

Mathematical Bridge. Legend says it was constructed on geometrical principles, but when taken apart for further investigation, it proved too complicated to rebuild without the help of the odd bolt or nail.

Further along, on the left, is Darwin College. **Darwin College** ④. Darwin, one of five Cambridge colleges for post-graduate students only, was founded in 1964. In the days before it became a college one of Charles Darwin's sons lived here, in the centre house. The book *Period Piece* by Gwen Raverat, grand-daughter of Darwin, was written here and describes life in this house during the 1880s.

After passing Darwin, continue across the traffic-lights and up Sidgwick Avenue to the Sidgwick Site on the right. **Sidgwick Site** ⑤. During the second half of the 19th century, student numbers increased rapidly and in the congested town centre it was impossible to find extra teaching space or accommodation. New colleges were therefore built to the west of the river (Newnham in 1875, Selwyn in 1882) as was extra housing for Dons who, after 1882, were permitted to marry. Further development of the area continued in the 20th century.

Turn right through the Sidgwick Site, under the walkway of the modern teaching blocks, to the Faculty of History. **Faculty of History** ⑥. Completed in 1968, this modern glass-faced building by James Stirling has caused more controversy than most. For some it is bold and exciting, for others brutal and without constraint. It has also suffered many problems such as leaking roofs and peeling tiles and brickwork. Despite all this, it remains one of the most eye-catching buildings of the modern University.

Continue along the footpath, crossing West Road on the playing fields of King's College School, to the University Library. **University Library** ⑦. In addition to college and faculty libraries, nearly every student spends some time amongst the four million books housed here. It is one of the few copyright libraries in the country entitled to receive, free, a copy of every book published in Britain. As a result, the 45 miles of shelving originally built in 1934 have already been considerably extended.

Turn right down Burrell's Walk, cross Queen's Road and follow the footpath to the right, along by the stream through the Backs. **The Backs** ⑧. It is unusual to find stretches of open meadow, pleasant walks and gardens so close to a city centre. This land is, however, owned by the colleges which 'back' onto the river. Two clearly distinguishable areas of raised ground opposite King's College are all that remains of a causeway that once crossed the river to a parish church standing where King's Lawn is today.

Turn left through the back gate of King's College, cross over the river and go through to the front entrance of the college to return to King's Parade.

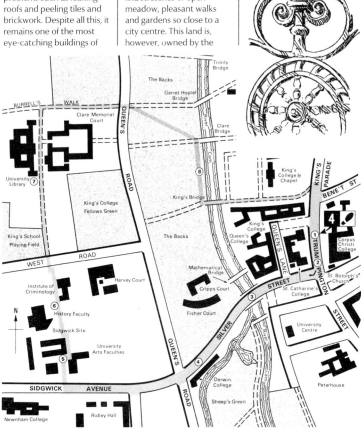

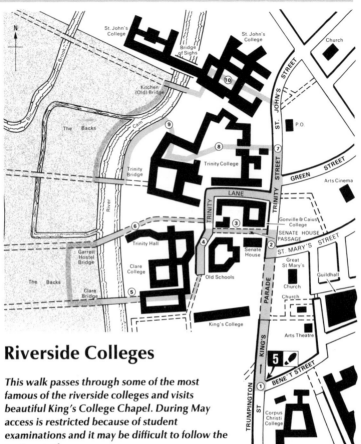

Riverside Colleges

This walk passes through some of the most famous of the riverside colleges and visits beautiful King's College Chapel. During May access is restricted because of student examinations and it may be difficult to follow the route exactly.

> *Allow 1½ hours*
> *Start at the King's Parade/ Bene't Street junction and walk along King's Parade towards the Senate House.*

King's Parade ①. This much-photographed street contains many oddments of interest as well as a wealth of history. King's College, with its Chapel, is the obvious focal-point—but outside, notice the post-box dating back to Victorian times. The buildings opposite have a mixture of styles and functions and are owned by various colleges. Above the shops is student accommodation, added to piecemeal over the years, hence the variety in height of the buildings. At the end of the row is Ryder and

Amis, an outfitters specialising in academic dress for all occasions. Displayed in the window are fixture lists for college matches. Great St Mary's Church, next door, is the University Church. The stone circle on the right-hand buttress is the point from which all distances locally are measured, and at one time all students had to live within three miles of this circle. **Senate House** ②. Built in the 1720s, this is one of the few purely classical buildings in Cambridge. It serves as a meeting place, debating chamber and stage for one of the University's most colourful ceremonies—Degree Day. It has also been the target of student pranks. One night a

car appeared on the roof of the Senate House—it took a week for the authorities to work out how to get it down.

Turn left down Senate House Passage. **Senate House Passage** ③. It is said the cobbles on the left are the property of the University, on the right of Gonville and Caius College, and the central slabs are the property of the town! Sundials crown the Gate of Honour (to the right), the final of the three 'gates' which a Caius student would pass through on his 'path' to a degree.

At the end of the passage turn left into Trinity Lane. **Trinity Lane** ④. At a time when Cambridge prospered on its river trade, this tiny lane was part of the main street of the town. However, when Henry VI decided to build his huge chapel at King's, he cleared a large part of central Cambridge, demolishing houses and interrupting the street-line.

Turn left through Clare College. **Clare College** ⑤. This college was re-founded by Elizabeth de Clare in 1338, when the original (1326) buildings were destroyed by fire. Some say the present style is more like a palace than a college. The bridge over the river is the oldest one remaining today.

Go right through the back gate of the college and right again to cross Garret Hostel Bridge. **Trinity Hall** ⑥. The gateway in Garret Hostel Lane once stood at the front of the college and was used as an alternative entrance at a time when much friction existed between 'town' and 'gown'. In peaceful periods the main gate was open, allowing horse and cart to enter, but if trouble arose, the smaller gate gave quick access to a man on horseback. During riots only the inner gate was opened leaving just enough room for a man to run in to the safety of the college.

Turn left into Trinity Lane, then right. At the junction, follow Trinity Street left to the main gate of Trinity College. **Trinity College** ⑦.

Founded by Henry VIII, Trinity College stands on the site of earlier colleges and hostels. One of these, King's Hall, was initiated by Edward III, and his coat of arms can be seen above the gate along with those of his six sons. One of these shields is blank, as this son died before the arms could be presented. The statue is of Henry VIII, the target of yet another student prank. In his hand is not a sceptre, but a chair leg! On the right of the gate is a small apple tree which is said to have been grown from the seedling of the tree that inspired Newton's theory of gravity. The rooms to the right of the gate are where Newton stayed whilst studying at Trinity.

Enter the Great Court. **Great Court** ⑧. This is the largest private enclosed court in the country and it is a college tradition to try to run around its perimeter before the clock strikes 12 (it takes 43 seconds). Lord Byron was a student at Trinity and is said to have taken baths in the fountain and kept a bear as a pet. Prince Charles also studied here.

Climb the steps on the far side of the court and go past the dining hall into Nevile's Court where the Wren Library can be seen. **Wren Library** ⑨. This fine example

LABEL STOP. KING'S

of Christopher Wren's work was begun in 1676. The four statues above it represent Divinity, Law, Physics and Mathematics—traditional subjects of the University. Inside the library, showcases include works by Newton and Milton, a first folio of Shakespeare, and a manuscript of *Winnie the Pooh*.

Leave by the back gate, walk left alongside the river and cross Trinity Bridge. Turn right and continue on the path, over a stream, then re-cross the river, via Kitchen Bridge, into St John's College grounds. **St John's College** ⑩. To the left of the river is New Court, built in neo-Gothic style in the late 1820s. Its shape, with the high central section, is often referred to as 'the wedding cake'. As you re-cross the river at Kitchen Bridge you can see the so-called Bridge of Sighs, built in 1831 to connect New Court with the older buildings. One year students floated a car upriver on four punts and, under cover of darkness, left it suspended beneath the bridge.

Follow the passage-way left into Third Court and right, through two more courts. Once out into St John's Street turn right down Trinity Street and King's Parade, to return to the start of the walk.

BRIDGE OF SIGHS

Newnham to Grantchester

This pleasant walk passes through the suburbs of Newnham and crosses the Cam's delightful river meadows, ending up at the well-known village of Grantchester beloved by Rupert Brooke.

Allow 1 hour (one-way). Start at the cross-roads where Queen's Road meets Silver Street. Walk south down Newnham Road, past the pond and over the roundabout, keeping the green, Lammas Land, on your left.

Lammas Land. The word 'Lammas' comes from the Old English, *llaf*, meaning loaf or bread, and *maesse*, meaning mass. Lammas Day, 1 August, was a harvest festival. From this date until early spring all Lammas Lands became open for the 'commoners' to graze their livestock upon. No one exercises this customary right now, but the area remains an open space to be used by the public at all times of year.

Newnham. This suburb of Cambridge was just a hamlet in pre-Conquest days, but was probably settled as early as Saxon times. It stood on slightly higher ground and was the site of a land grant for a Carmelite friary in about 1250. Prior to that, the *Domesday Book* records the existence of a mill, which reflects the importance of Cambridge as an inland port. Field paths would have connected Newnham to Cambridge. By the end of the 15th century the Carmelites had moved closer to the town, and Newnham remained a small settlement until the expansion of the University in the late 19th century. It is now considered to be one of the more desirable areas of Cambridge in which to live.

Continue down Grantchester Street. At the end follow the signpost to the footpath which runs alongside the river to

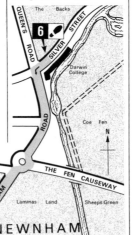

Grantchester. **Grantchester Meadows**. The riverside meadows are a popular place, especially in summer, for an easy stroll to Grantchester village. Although commonly known as the Cam, an earlier name for the river was the Granta. The name is Celtic in origin, probably meaning 'fen river' or 'muddy river', which it

certainly is. In season, punts pass up and down the river, though for the inexperienced this method of transport can often prove harder work, and more hazardous, than walking. As you look back towards Cambridge, the pinnacles of King's College Chapel and other landmarks are visible above the treeline.

Go through the gate at the end of the footpath, along the lane, then turn left and follow the road around the bend, past The Old Vicarage. **The Old Vicarage**. This is the setting of the famous poem by Rupert Brooke, written in 1912. A student and later Fellow at King's College, he left his lodgings there to live at The Orchard, and later moved to The Old Vicarage as a paying guest in 1910.

Follow the footpath along the side of the house to the mill pond. **Grantchester Mill**. The river here was once busy with barges travelling upriver to the mill. However, the original building was destroyed by fire in 1928 and has been rebuilt as a house. Only punts now venture this far, and it is a peaceful spot for anglers, visitors and aspiring poets!

Turn right, following the road back to the village and the church. **Parish Church**. A church has stood on this site since the 11th century, when Grantchester was a tiny village built on the higher ground above the river. As in other settlements, it was the focal point of village life. The present building dates from the late 14th century and is particularly noted for its fine chancel. In the churchyard a war memorial bears the name of Rupert Brooke, amongst others.

Continue through the village, returning to Cambridge either by road or back along the footpath. Alternatively, by planning ahead, a bus can be taken back to the city centre.

AA

Pocket Guide to

CAMBRIDGE

Using the Directory

ABBREVIATIONS

approx—approximately
appt—appointment
BH—Bank Holiday(s)
Chr—Christmas
EH—English Heritage—
buildings in the care of the
Historic Buildings and
Monuments Commission
(used to be known as
Ancient Monuments (AM))
ER—Egon Ronay (see below)
Etr—Easter
eve—evening
ex—excluding/except
ext—extension
gps—groups
hr—hour(s)
incl—including/inclusive
m—mile(s)
nr—near
NT—National Trust—
Regional Office, Blickling,
Norwich ☎ *Aylsham*
(0263) 733471/734077
☎—telephone
TIC—Tourist Information
Centre—addresses and
phone numbers in Useful
Information section
wk—week(s)
wknd—weekend(s)

TELEPHONE NUMBERS (☎)

Phone numbers are on the
Cambridge exchange (STD
code 0223) if no other
exchange name or number is
given. If just an exchange
number is given the exchange
name is the same as the entry
name.

AA CLASSIFICATIONS
Hotels

★ Good hotels and
inns, generally of
small scale and
with good
furnishings and
facilities.
★★ Hotels with
a higher
standard of
accommodation.

There should be
20% private
bathrooms or
showers.
★★★ Well-appointed
hotels. Two-
thirds of the
bedrooms
should have
private
bathrooms or
showers.
★★★★ Exceptionally
well-appointed
hotels offering
high standards of
comfort and
service. All
bedrooms
should have
private
bathrooms or
showers.
★★★★★ Luxury hotels
offering the
highest
international
standards.

Restaurants

✕ Modest but good
restaurant.
✕✕ Restaurant
offering a higher
standard of
comfort than
above.
✕✕✕ Well-appointed
restaurant.
✕✕✕✕ Exceptionally
well-appointed
restaurant.
✕✕✕✕✕ Luxury restaurant.

Camp sites

▶ Site licence; 10%
of pitches for
touring units; site
density not more
than 30 per acre;
2 separate toilets
for each sex per
30 pitches; good
quality tapwater;
efficient waste
disposal; regular

cleaning of
ablutions block;
fire precautions;
well-drained
ground.
▶▶ All one-pennant
facilities plus: 2
washbasins with
hot and cold
water for each
sex per 30
pitches in
separate
washrooms;
warden available
at certain times
of the day.
▶▶▶ All two-pennant
facilities plus:
one shower or
bath for each sex
per 30 pitches,
with hot and
cold water;
electric shaver
points and
mirrors; all-night
lighting of toilet
blocks; deep
sinks for washing
clothes; facilities
for buying milk,
bread and gas;
warden present
during day, on
call by night.

EGON RONAY

Egon Ronay appointed
establishments are indicated
by (ER).

AA AND ER GUIDES

For more details on the
establishments listed, see the
AA guides: *Hotels and
Restaurants in Britain;
Guesthouses, Farmhouses and
Inns in Britain; Holiday Homes,
Cottages and Apartments in
Britain* and *Camping and
Caravanning in Britain*, and the
ER guides: *Healthy Eating Out;
Pub Guide; Just a Bite* and
*Egon Ronay's Guide to Hotels,
Restaurants and Inns.*

---

*The information in this Directory is liable to change at short notice. While every effort has
been made to ensure that it is comprehensive and up to date, the publishers cannot accept
responsibility for errors or omissions, or for changes in the details given.*

Accommodation

Visitors to Cambridge should remember that accommodation is likely to be difficult to find during 'May Week', the Degree Ceremony and the Cambridge Festival. They should book well ahead, particularly at these times.

HOTELS—The AA's choice

★ ★ ★ ★**Garden House**
Granta Place, off Mill Lane (Best Western) ☎63421 Telex no 81463

★ ★ ★ ★**Post House**
Lakeview, Bridge Road, Impington (2½m N, on N side roundabout junction A45/B1049) (Trusthouse Forte) ☎Histon (022 023) 7000 Telex no 817123

★ ★ ★ ★**University Arms**
Regent Street (Inter Hotel) ☎351241 Telex no 817311

★ ★ ★**Cambridgeshire Moat House** (Queens Moat) Bar Hill ☎Crafts Hill (0954) 80555 Telex no 817141

★ ★ ★**Gonville** Gonville Place ☎66611

★ ★**Arundel House**
53 Chesterton Road ☎67701 Telex no 817936

★**Quy Mill** Newmarket Road, Stow-cum-Quy ☎Teversham (022 05) 4114

GUESTHOUSES

Antwerp 36 Brookfields ☎247690

Ayeone Cleave 95 Gilbert Road ☎63387

Belle Vue 33 Chesterton Road ☎351859

Fairways 143 Cherry Hinton Road ☎246063

Hamilton Hotel 156 Chesterton Road ☎65664

Helen's Hotel 167 – 169 Hills Road ☎246465

Lensfield Hotel 53 Lensfield Road ☎355017

Sorrento Hotel 196 Cherry Hinton Road ☎243533

Suffolk House Private Hotel
69 Milton Road ☎352016

SELF CATERING

20 Water Street (house), Old Chesterton. For bookings contact Mrs S J Mackay, 'Roebuck House', 28 Ferry Lane, Chesterton, Cambridge ☎60000

Whitehouse Holiday Apartments (flats), Conduit Head Road ☎67110 & Madingley (0954) 211361 (1½m from centre of Cambridge, just off the A1303)

CAMP SITES

▶▶▶**Highfield Farm Camping Site** Long Road, Comberton ☎(022 026) 2308 (3m W of Cambridge between A45 and A603. From M11 leave junction 12, take A603 ½m then B1046 to Comberton)

Eating & Drinking Out

Angeline (ER), 8 Market Passage ☎60305
Closed Sun eve, BH & 3 wk Etr

Charlie Chan (ER), 14 Regent Street ☎61763
Closed 25 & 26 Dec.
Chinese cooking

Nettles (ER), 6 St Edwards Passage, King's Parade
Closed Sun & BH.
Wholefood vegetarian

✕ **Peking** 21 Burleigh Street ☎354755
Pekinese cooking

Upstairs (ER), 71 Castle Street ☎312569
Closed Mon & 25 & 26 Dec

Waffles (ER), 71 Castle Street ☎312569
Closed Mon, 2 wk Sep & 1 wk Chr

Places to Visit

ANCIENT MONUMENTS AND BUILDINGS

See also under Open-air attractions for village reconstructions, etc.

Bury St Edmunds—Abbey ruins (EH). Free

Castle Hedingham—Hedingham Castle ☎Hedingham (0787) 60261.
Open Etr, May – Oct daily, 10 – 5. Gps at other times by appt

Denny Abbey (EH), Ely Road, Waterbeach (5m NE Cambridge).
Open mid Mar – mid Oct, Wed – Sat, 9.30 – 6.30, Sun 2 – 6.30; mid Oct – mid Mar, Sat 9.30 – 4, Sun 2 – 4

Royston Cave Melbourn Street.
Open Etr – Sep, Sat, Sun & BH Mon, 2 – 6

Saffron Walden Maze.
Open all year. Free

Thetford Priory (EH).
Open all year. Free

Thorney Abbey Church (7m NE Peterborough).
Open all year. Free

Weeting—Grimes Graves (EH) (2m N Brandon) ☎Thetford (0842) 810656.
Open mid Mar – mid Oct, Mon – Sat 9.30 – 6.30, Sun 2 – 6.30; mid Oct – mid Mar, Mon – Sat 9.30 – 4, Sun 2 – 4

Widdington (4m S Saffron Walden)—Priors Hall Barn (EH).
Open late Mar – late Sep, Sat, Sun & BH, 9.30 – 6.30

ART GALLERIES IN CAMBRIDGE

Cambridge Holographics 29 Magdalene Street ☎470349. Open Mon–Sat 10–6, Sun 10.30–6

Fitzwilliam Museum Trumpington Street ☎332900. Upper galleries (paintings) open Tue–Sat 2–5, Sun 2.15–5. Also Etr, Spring & Aug BH Mons. Closed Good Fri & 24 Dec–1 Jan (incl). Free

Kettle's Yard Northampton Street/Castle Street ☎352124. Permanent Collection and house open daily 2–4. Exhibition gallery open Tue–Sat 12.30–5.30 (7pm Thu), Sun 2–5.30. Closed BH & Chr–New Year incl. Gps of 10 or more admitted to Permanent Collection by appt only. Free

ART GALLERIES OUTSIDE CAMBRIDGE

Many of the region's historic houses (see under that heading) also have fine art collections, as do some of the museums such as Lavenham Little Hall.

Bedford—Cecil Higgins Art Gallery & Museum, Castle Close ☎(0234) 211222. Open Tue–Fri & BH Mon 12.30–5, Sat 11–5, Sun 2–5. Closed Good Fri & Chr. Free

Bury St Edmunds Art Gallery. Open Tue–Sat 10.30–4.30. Sun by prior arrangement

Peterborough—City Museum & Art Gallery, Priestgate ☎(0733) 43329. Open Oct–Apr, Tue–Sat 12–5; May–Sep, Tue–Sat 10–5. Closed Good Fri & Chr. Free

Sudbury—Gainsborough Museum (see under Museums)

CHURCHES AND CATHEDRALS IN CAMBRIDGE

Fuller details, including the locations, of the Cambridge churches listed below are given in the city gazetteer section (see pages 42 to 64).

All Saints Church (disused)

Great St Mary's Church. Small admission charge for tower

Holy Trinity Church

Little St Mary's Church

Our Lady and the English Martyrs Roman Catholic Church

Round Church

St Andrew the Great Church (disused and only visible from outside)

St Bene't's Church

St Botolph's Church

St Edward's Church

St Giles' Church—now houses Brass Rubbing Centre (see Crafts entry in Shopping section)

St Michael's Church

St Peter's Church

Stourbridge Chapel—Key available (see chapel notice board)

CATHEDRALS OUTSIDE CAMBRIDGE

Ely Cathedral Open winter 7.30–6.30, summer 7–7. (Admission charge)

Peterborough Cathedral

COLLEGES AND UNIVERSITY BUILDINGS

Fuller details, including the locations, of the Cambridge colleges listed below are given in the city gazetteer section; however, the century of foundation of the college—not always the date of the oldest buildings—is given here as a rough guide. In general the colleges are open to visitors between 9am and 5.30pm, but it should be remembered that they are private property and the public have no automatic rights to visit them. The libraries, dining halls and gardens tend to have much more restricted (if any) opening hours, and only those open to the public on a regular basis are included here. The colleges are closed to the public during examination time—May–mid June. Parties of 10 or more people wishing to visit the colleges must be accompanied by a Blue Badged Cambridge Guide—contact the Tourist Information Centre for details.

Christ's College (15C)

Churchill College (20C)

Clare College (14C). Fellows' Garden open Mon–Fri 2–4.45

Corpus Christi College (14C)

Darwin College (20C)

Downing College (19C)

Emmanuel College (16C)

Fitzwilliam College (20C)

Girton College (19C)

Gonville and Caius College (14C)

Jesus College (15C). Chapel open 6am–10pm

King's College (15C). Chapel normally open term-time Mon–Sat 9–3.45 & Sun 2–3, 4.30–5.45; vacations Mon–Sat 9–5, Sun 10.30–5. Choral services term-time 5.30 (Tue–Sat) & 10.30 & 3.30 (Sun)

Magdalene College (16C). Pepys Library open Mon–Sat 2.30–3.30 (Oct–Dec & Jan–Mar term-times), 11.30–12.30 & 2.30–3.30 (Apr (term-time)—late Aug)

New Hall (20C)

Newnham College (19C)

Pembroke College (14C)

Peterhouse (13C)

Queens' College (15C). Open 1.45–4.30 (small admission charge)

Robinson College (20C)

St Catharine's College (15C)

St John's College (16C). Chapel normally open term-time Tue–Fri 9–12 & 2–4, Sat & Mon 9–12. Services during term-time Tue–Sat 6.30, Sun 10.30 & 6.30

Selwyn College (19C)

Sidney Sussex College (16C)

Trinity College (16C). Wren Library open Mon–Fri 12–2 & Sat (term-time only) 10.30–12.30, closed BH. Chapel services during term-time Sun 6.15 & Wed 6.30

Trinity Hall (14C)

University Library—guided tours 3pm Mon–Fri

Westminster College (19C)

Wolfson College (20C)

GARDENS IN CAMBRIDGE

Botanic Garden. Entrances on Hills Road, Bateman Street and Trumpington Road. Open Mon – Sat 8 – 6.30 (or dusk if earlier), Sun May – Sep 2.30 – 6.30 (or dusk). Glasshouses open 11 – 12.30 & 2 – 4. Free

Clare College—Fellows' Garden (see under Colleges)

GARDENS OUTSIDE CAMBRIDGE

Many of the historic houses in the area (see section below) have fine gardens. Unless stated otherwise the gardens are open at the same time as the house.

Buckden Palace. Gardens open May – Aug 10 – 6, Sep – Apr 10 – 4. Interior open Jun – Aug, Tue, 2.30 – 5. Free

Finchingfield—Spains Hall. Open May – Jul Sun & May BH 2 – 5

Saffron Walden—Bridge End Gardens ☎Great Dunmow (0371) 5411. Open all year daily 9 – dusk. Free

HISTORIC HOUSES AND CASTLES

Anglesey Abbey (NT), Lode (6m NE Cambridge) ☎811200. House open mid Apr – mid Oct, Wed – Sun & BH, 1.30 – 5.30. Gardens open Apr – Jun, Wed – Sun, late Jun – Oct daily, 1.30 – 5.30. Times may vary slightly from year to year. Separate entrance fee for gardens only available. (See also Lode Watermill under Open-air attractions)

Audley End House (EH) (nr Saffron Walden) ☎Saffron Walden (0799) 22399. House open Etr – Sep, Tue – Sun 1 – 5, grounds 12 – 6.30 (& also most of Oct). Also BH Mon

Buckden Palace (see under Gardens outside Cambridge)

Burghley House (1m SE Stamford) ☎Stamford (0780) 52451. Open Etr – Oct daily 11 – 5, Good Fri 2 – 5. Usually closed for one day in early Sep

Euston Hall (3m S Thetford) ☎Thetford (0842) 66366. Open early Jun – late Sep, Thu 2.30 – 5.30

Halstead—Gosfield Hall. Open May – Sep Wed & Thu 2 – 5 with guided tours (obligatory) at 2.30 & 3.15

Hinchingbrooke House (1½m W Huntingdon) ☎Huntingdon (0480) 51121. Open Apr – Aug, Sun & BH Mon 1 – 5. Gps by appt at other times

Ickworth (NT), Horringer (3m SW Bury St Edmunds). ☎Horringer (028 488) 270. Open May – Sep daily (ex Mon & Thu) & BH Mon 1.30 – 5.30. Apr & Oct wknd only. Park open daily dawn to dusk

Kimbolton Castle (7m NW St Neots) ☎Huntingdon (0480) 860505. Open Etr, Spring BH wknd & mid Jul – Aug Sun 2 – 6

Lavenham—The Priory, Water Street ☎(0787) 247417. Open daily (ex Sun) Etr – Oct 10.30 – 12.30 & 2 – 5.30

Long Melford—Kentwell Hall ☎Sudbury (0787) 310207. Open Etr Fri – Tue then Etr – mid Jun, Wed, Thu, Sun 2 – 6; mid Jun – mid Jul, Sat & Sun only 11 – 5 (historical re-creations); mid Jul – Sep, Wed – Sun 2 – 6. Admission fee for gardens and animals only available

Long Melford—Melford Hall (NT). Open early Apr – late Sep, Wed, Thu, Sun & BH Mon, & Sat Jun – Aug 2 – 6

Longthorpe Tower (EH) (2m W Peterborough). Open mid Mar – mid Oct, Tue & Sun 2 – 6.30, Wed – Sat 9.30 – 6.30; mid Oct – mid Mar as summer but closes at 4pm

Oxborough—Oxburgh Hall (NT) (7m SW Swaffham). ☎Gooderstone (036 621) 258. Open May – Sep daily (ex Thu & Fri) 1.30 – 5.30, BH Mon 11 – 5.30. Also late Apr & early Oct Sat & Sun 1.30 – 5.30

Wimpole Hall (NT) (8m SW Cambridge) ☎207257. Open mid Apr – late Oct daily (ex Mon & Fri), 1 – 5 & BH Mon. Home Farm open from 11

Wisbech—Peckover House (NT), North Brink ☎(0945) 583463. Open May – Sep, Sat – Wed & also late Apr & early Oct Sat, Sun & BH Mon, 2 – 5.30. Gps by appt

MILITARY CEMETERY

Madingley (4m W Cambridge)—American Military Cemetery ☎(0954) 210350. Open May – Sep 8 – 6, Oct – Apr 9 – dusk

MUSEUMS IN CAMBRIDGE

Many of the museums listed here are attached to University departments. Their opening hours tend to be limited so check times carefully to avoid a wasted journey.

Fitzwilliam Museum Trumpington Street ☎332900. Open Tue – Sat (Lower galleries 10 – 2, Upper galleries 2 – 5); Sun (all galleries) 2.15 – 5. Also Etr, Spring & Aug BH Mons. Closed Good Fri & 24 Dec – 1 Jan (incl). Free

Folk Museum Castle Street ☎355159. Open Tue – Sat 10.30 – 5, Sun 2.30 – 4.30 (closed BH). Opening times subject to revision

Museum of Archaeology and Anthropology Downing Street ☎333510. Open Mon – Fri 2 – 4, Sat 10 – 12.30. Closed Etr wk, 24 Dec – 1 Jan (incl) & some BH. Free

Museum of Classical Archaeology Sidgwick Avenue ☎335153. Open Mon – Fri 9 – 1, 2.15 – 5; Sat (term-time only) 9 – 1. Closed Chr & Etr. Free

Museum of Technology Riverside (off Newmarket Road) ☎68650. Open first Sun in every month, 2 – 6 (static). Pumping engine in steam approx 5 wknd during year, dates from TIC

Museum of Zoology Downing Street ☎336600. Open Mon – Fri 2.15 – 4.45. Closed Etr, Chr & BH. Student gps at other times by appt. Free

Scott Polar Research Institute Lensfield Road ☎336540. Open all year Mon–Sat 2.30–4. Closed some BH. Free

Sedgwick Museum of Geology Downing Street ☎333400. Open all year Mon–Fri 9–1, 2–5; Sat (term-time only) 10–1. Closed Chr & some BH

Whipple Museum of the History of Science Free School Lane ☎334540. Open Mon–Fri 2–4 (closed BH & university vacations). Also open first Sun in the month all year. Free

MUSEUMS OUTSIDE CAMBRIDGE

Ashwell—Village Museum, Swan Street ☎(046 274) 2155. Open Sun & BH 2.30–5. Gps by appt at other times

Bedford Museum Castle Lane ☎(0234) 53323. Open all year Tue–Sat 11–5, Sun 2–5. Closed Mon (ex BH afternoons), Good Fri & Chr. Free

Bedford—Bunyan Museum, Mill Street ☎(0234) 58870/58627. Open Apr–Sep, Tue–Sat 2–4

Bedford—Cecil Higgins Art Gallery & Museum (see under Art galleries)

Bedford—Elstow Moot Hall (1½m SW) ☎(0234) 66889. Open Apr–Oct, Tue–Sat & BH 2–5, Sun 2–5.30

Bishop's Stortford—Rhodes Memorial Museum and Commonwealth Centre, South Road ☎(0279) 51746. Open Mon & Wed–Sat 10–4, Tue 10–12. Closed early Aug, Sun & BH

Bury St Edmunds—Gershom-Parkington Collection of Clocks & Watches, Angel Corner, Angel Hill ☎(0284) 63233 ext 227. Open Mon–Sat 10–5, Sun 2–5. Closed Chr, New Year & Good Fri. Free

Bury St Edmunds—Moyses Hall Museum, Cornhill ☎(0284) 63233 ext 236. Open Mar–Oct, Mon–Sat 10–1, 2–5; Nov–Feb, Mon–Sat 10–1, 2–4. Closed winter BH, Good Fri, Etr Sat & May Day BH

Bury St Edmunds—Suffolk Regiment Museum, Gibraltar Barracks, Out Risbygate ☎(0284) 2394. Open Mon–Fri 10–12, 2–4. Closed BH and occasionally at other times. Free

Cavendish—Sue Ryder Foundation Museum ☎Glemsford (0787) 280252. Open Mon–Sat 10–5.30, Sun 10–11 & 12.15–5.30

Chatteris Museum Grove House, High Street ☎(03543) 2414. Open Thu 2–4 and by appt. Free

Clare—Ancient House Museum, High Street ☎(0787) 277865. Open mid Apr–mid Oct, Wed–Sun & BH 2.30–4.30, Sun 11–12.30

Ely Museum Sacrist's Gate, High Street ☎(0353) 2516. Open Oct–May, Sat & Sun 2–4.15; Jun–Sep, Thu, Sat & Sun 2–5. Visits at other times by appt

Ely—Stained Glass Museum, Ely Cathedral ☎(0353) 5103. Open Mar–Oct, Mon–Fri 10.30–4, Sat & BH 10.30–4.30, Sun 12–3

Finchingfield—Guildhall & Museum. Open Etr–Sep, Sun & BH 2.30–6.30. Free

Halstead—Brewery Chapel Museum, Adams Court. Open Apr–Oct, Sat 10–12.30, 2–4.30, Sun 2–4.30. Free

Hinchingbrooke House (see under Historic houses)

Huntingdon—Cromwell Museum, Grammar School Walk ☎(0480) 425830. Open Nov–Mar, Tue–Fri 2–5, Sat 11–1, 2–4, Sun 2–4; Apr–Oct, Tue–Fri 11–1, 2–5, Sat & Sun 11–1, 2–4. Closed Chr wk & BH ex Good Fri. Free

King's Lynn—Lynn Museum, Market Street ☎(0553) 775001. Open Mon–Sat 10–5. Closed BH, Chr & New Year

King's Lynn–Museum of Social History, 27 King Street ☎(0553) 775004. Open Tue–Sat 10–5. Closed BH, Chr & New Year

King's Lynn—Regalia Rooms, Trinity Guildhall. Heritage Centre open Apr–Oct, Mon–Sat 10–4. Other exhibitions open all year 10–4

King's Lynn–St George's Guildhall (NT), King Street. Open Mon–Fri 10.30–5, Sat 10–12.30 (ex when rehearsals in progress). Closed Good Fri, Chr & New Year. Free

Lavenham—Guildhall (NT). Open early Apr–Oct daily 11–1 & 2–5.30

Lavenham—Little Hall, Market Place ☎ (0787) 247179. Open Etr–mid Oct, Sat, Sun & BH 2.30–6 or by appt

March—March & District Museum, High Street ☎ (0354) 55300. Open Wed 10–12, Sat 10–12, 2–4. Gps by appt. Free

Mildenhall Museum King Street. Open Wed–Sun 2.30–4.30 (Fri 11–4.30). Free

Newmarket—National Horse-Racing Museum, 99 High Street ☎ (0638) 667333. Open late Mar–early Dec, Tue–Sat, BH Mon & Mon in Aug 10–5, Sun 2–5

Peterborough—City Museum & Art Gallery, Priestgate ☎ (0733) 43329. Open Oct–Apr, Tue–Sat 12–5; May–Sep, Tue–Sat 10–5. Closed Good Fri & Chr. Free

Royston Museum Lower King Street ☎ (0763) 42587. Open Wed & Sat 10–5. Free

Saffron Walden Museum Museum Street ☎ (0799) 22494. Open Tue–Sat 10–5 (4pm Oct–Mar), Sun & BH 2.30–5. Closed Good Fri & 24/25 Dec. Free

St Ives—Norris Library & Museum, The Broadway ☎(0480) 65101. Open Oct–Apr, Tue–Fri 10–1, 2–4, Sat 10–12; May–Sep, Tue–Fri 10–1, 2–5, Sat 10–12, 2–5. Closed BH wknd. Gps at other times by appt. Free

St Neots—Longsands Museum, Longsands Road ☎Huntingdon (0480) 72740. By appt only during school opening hours. Free

Sudbury—Gainsborough Museum, Gainsborough Street ☎(0787) 72958. Open Tue–Sat 10–5, Sun & BH Mon 2–5. Closed Good Fri & Chr–New Year, & at 4pm Oct–mid Apr

Thaxted—Guildhall, Town Street. Open Etr–Sep, Sun 2–6; BH wknd, Sat–Mon 11–6, also Good Fri 2–6

Thetford—Ancient House Museum, White Hart Street ☎(0842) 2599. Open Mon–Sat 10–5 (closed Mon 1–2); Sun 2–5 (late May–late Sep only). Closed Good Fri, Chr & New Year

Whittlesey—Whittlesea Museum, Market Street ☎Turves (073 120) 280. Open Fri & Sun 2.30–4.30, Sat 10–12. Closed BH

Wisbech—Wisbech & Fenland Museum, Museum Square ☎(0945) 583817. Open Tue–Sat 10–4 (10–5 Apr–Sep). Closed BH. Free

NATURE RESERVES AND TRAILS

CAMBIENT—contact Cambridge and Isle of Ely Naturalists' Trust, 5 Fulbourn Manor, Manor Walk, Fulbourn ☎880788 for details of reserves in Cambridgeshire

Sandy—RSPB reserve. Open daily

Welney Wildfowl Refuge, nr March ☎Ely (0353) 860711. Open daily 10–5 (ex Chr). Gp visits for early evening in winter bookable in advance.

Wicken Fen (NT) ☎Ely (0353) 720274. Open daily. Parties by appt only

Nature trails: Clare Castle Country Park, Grafham Water, Hatfield Forest and Wandlebury

OPEN-AIR ATTRACTIONS

See also under Gardens, Nature reserves, Vineyards and Zoos.

Audley End Miniature Railway. Open Apr–Sep, Sat, Sun & BH Mon & daily (ex Mon) during school holidays, 2–6

Cockley Cley—Iceni Village & Museum (3m SW Swaffham) ☎Swaffham (0760) 21339. Open Etr–Oct daily 2–5.30; mid Jul–mid Sep daily 11.30–5.30. Gps by appt

Colne Valley Railway, Castle Hedingham Station (4m NW Halstead) ☎Hedingham (0787) 61174. Static displays open daily (ex 24 Dec–Feb) 11–5. Gps by appt in evenings. Steam days Etr–Oct, 1st & 3rd Sun of month & BH Sun & Mon, 12–5

Duxford—Imperial War Museum, Duxford Airfield (8m S Cambridge) ☎833963. Open mid Mar–early Nov daily (ex Good Fri & May Day BH) 10.30–5.30 (last admission 4.45 or dusk). Occasional flying days, dates from TIC or ☎835000

Great Gransden Post Mill (10m W Cambridge off B1046) Open Apr–Oct 9–6. Details of key holders from Post Office.

Haddenham—Farmland Museum, High Street ☎Ely (0353) 740381. Open first Sun each month 2–5 & each Wed 10–5 from May–Oct

Houghton Mill (NT) (2m from Huntingdon). Open mid Apr–mid Sep daily (ex Thu & Fri), mid Sep–mid Oct Sat & Sun only, 2–5.30

Lode Watermill (NT). Open mid Apr–mid Oct, wknd & BH Mon 1.30–5.30. Included in Anglesey Abbey admission fee. Corn grinding demonstrations on BH Mon & first Sun of month

Mildenhall Air Show. Contact TIC for details and dates.

Nene Valley Railway Museum, Wansford Station, Stibbington (7m W Peterborough) ☎Stamford (0780) 782854. Please phone or contact TIC for details of opening times and train running times

Old Warden (nr Biggleswade)—Shuttleworth Collection of Historic Aeroplanes and Cars ☎Northill (076 727) 288. Open daily 10.30–5.30 (last admission 4.30). Closed 1 wk at Chr

Ramsey Rural Museum, The Woodyard ☎ (0487) 813223. Open Apr–Sep, Sun 2–5. Free

Peterborough—East of England Show at Showground, Alwalton, in July ☎ (0733) 234451

Sacrewell Mill and Grassyard Collection, Thornhaugh (8m W Peterborough off A47) ☎Stamford (0780) 782222. Open late Apr–mid Oct, Sun 2–6. Gps by appt at other times

Stansted Mountfitchet—Mountfitchet Castle ☎ Bishop's Stortford (0279) 813237. Open daily mid Mar–mid Nov, 10–5

Stansted Mountfitchet—Windmill ☎ Bishop's Stortford (0279) 812096. Open 2.30–6.30 Apr–Oct first Sun in month & all Sun in Aug. Also Etr, May, Spring & Aug BH Sun & Mon. Other times by prior appt

Stowmarket—Museum of East Anglian Life ☎ (0449) 612229. Open late Mar–late Oct, Mon–Sat 11–5, Sun 12–5 (Jun–Aug 12–6)

Stretham Beam Engine, nr Ely. Open daily 9–6

Thaxted— John Webb's Windmill ☎(0371) 830366. Open May–Sep, Sat, Sun & BH, 2–6

West Stow Anglo-Saxon Village (7m NW Bury St Edmunds) ☎Culford (028 484) 718. Open Apr–Oct, Tue–Sat 2–5, Sun & BH 11–1 & 2–5. Surrounding parkland open 9–1hr before sunset. Gps by prior appt

Wimpole Hall (NT)—Home Farm. Open mid Apr–late Oct, 11–5 daily (ex Mon & Fri)

VINEYARDS

Cavendish—Nether Hall Manor ☎Glemsford (0787) 280221. Open all year daily, 11–4

Felsted Vineyards, Cricks Green ☎Chelmsford (0245) 361504. Open all year by appt

Linton—Chilford Hundred Vineyard, Balsham Road ☎892641.
Open May–Sep, Tue–Sat 10–5, Sun 11–5. Gps by appt at other times

ZOOS AND ANIMAL COLLECTIONS

See also the farm museums listed under Open-air attractions.

Kilverstone Wildlife Park (1m E Thetford) ☎Thetford (0842) 5369.
Open daily 10–6.30 (or dusk in winter)

Linton Zoo Hadstock Road ☎891308.
Open daily (ex 25 Dec) 10–7 (or dusk). Last admission ½hr before closing

Long Melford—Kentwell Hall (rare breeds) see under Historic houses

Norton Tropical Bird Gardens (7m E Bury St Edmunds) ☎Pakenham (0359) 30957.
Open all year daily 11–6 or dusk

Peakirk (Wildfowl Trust) (5m N Peterborough) ☎(0733) 252271.

Open daily (ex 24 & 25 Dec), 9.30–5.30 (or dusk Nov–Mar); also Sep–Apr first Mon in month to 7.30pm

Shepreth—Willers Mill Fish Farm and Animal Sanctuary, Station Road ☎Royston (0763) 61832.
Open Mar–Nov, 10.30–6.30 (or dusk)

Widdington (nr Newport)—Mole Hall Wildlife Park ☎Saffron Walden (0799) 40400.
Open mid Mar–early Nov 10.30–6 daily

Entertainment

Besides the entertainments listed below there are concerts, theatre, films, dances, etc. at festivals and special events both within and outside Cambridge. The local Tourist Information Centres (see Useful Information section) or in Cambridge the City Amenities and Recreation Department (☎358977) can supply full details.

Bury St Edmunds Festival (May)

Bury St Edmunds—various music recitals, films, concerts, etc. at the Art Gallery ☎(0284) 62081

Cambridge—'May Week' events (early Jun)

Cambridge Festival and Cambridge Folk Festival (late Jul). Details available May onwards ☎358977

King's Lynn Festival (late Jul–Aug, based at Fermoy Centre)

Long Melford—Kentwell Hall (historic re-creations mid Jun–mid Jul wknd, and other events during year—☎Sudbury (0787) 310207)

Tickets for a variety of local events may be obtained from the Cambridge Box Office at the Corn Exchange, Wheeler Street ☎357851.

BINGO

Coral Social Club 21 Hobson Street ☎356630

CINEMA

Arts Cinema Market Passage ☎352001

Cannon 1 & 2 St Andrew's Street ☎64537

Victoria 1 & 2 Market Hill ☎352677 (recorded messages—programmes) or 60061 (other enquiries)

DANCING

Cambridge has a number of groups specialising in particular types of dance (e.g. Scottish, Morris, Country) most of whom would welcome visitors to their meetings (details from TIC). The Cambridge International Club, 4a Downing Place ☎352384 organises Mon evening folk dances for student visitors.

Dinner dances:
Cambridgeshire Moat House Bar Hill, nr Cambridge ☎Crafts Hill (0954) 80555 (all year)

Garden House Hotel Granta Place ☎63421 (Nov & Dec)

The University Arms Hotel Regent Street ☎351241 (Nov–Apr)

The University Centre Granta Place ☎63365 (Dec)

DISCOS AND LIVE BANDS

Ronelles International Heidelberg Gardens, Lion Yard ☎64222 (disco diner)

Route 66 Wheeler Street ☎357503 (disco diner)

Sea Cadet Hall Riverside (live bands most Sat evenings)

MUSIC—CLASSICAL

Cambridge Symphony Orchestra Details of concerts ☎65374

Cambridge University Music School West Road ☎335176. Concerts during term-time. Details from Music School, TIC or Public Library.

Corn Exchange concerts see TIC for details or ☎357851

MacKenzie Society concerts at Carpenter Hall, Victoria Street, Tue (term-time) 7.45pm ☎Histon (022 023) 2915

MUSIC IN CAMBRIDGE PUBS

The Alma Russell Court (off Russell Street) ☎64965 (Sat—rhythm & blues)

The Burleigh Arms Newmarket Road ☎316881 (live bands regularly, Sun lunchtime—jazz)

The Cambridge Arms King Street ☎359650 (Mon—various, Tue & Sun—jazz)

The Geldart 1 Ainsworth Street ☎355983 (Tue & Sun—folk)

The Man on the Moon Norfolk Street ☎350610 (Mon—traditional jazz, Wed—mainstream, Fri—modern jazz, Sat—country & western)

The Salisbury Arms Tenison Road ☎60363 (occasional Sun lunchtime—jazz)

NIGHT CLUBS

Newmarket—The Cabaret Club, 146 High Street ☎(0638) 668601

THEATRES IN CAMBRIDGE

ADC Theatre Park Street

☎352001 (Box Office) or 359547 (general)

Arts Theatre Peas Hill ☎352000 (Box Office) or 355246 (general)

Mumford Theatre (CCAT), East Road ☎352932

THEATRES OUTSIDE CAMBRIDGE

Bury St Edmunds—Theatre Royal

☎(0284) 5127

King's Lynn—Fermoy Centre ☎(0553) 774725

Peterborough—Key Theatre ☎(0733) 52437

Sudbury—Quay Theatre ☎(0787) 74745

Wisbech—Angles Theatre ☎(0945) 63607

Sports & Recreation

GENERAL

Details are given below of the main venues for spectator sports, as well as facilities available for public use in Cambridge. Where certain sports facilities are not available in the city, those in other nearby towns are mentioned. The Eastern Council for Sport and Recreation, 26 Bromham Road, Bedford ☎(0234) 45222 can supply further information about the availability of sports facilities and coaching courses, as can the City Amenities and Recreation Department (☎358977) in Cambridge itself.

Use of tennis courts and bowling greens can usually be arranged on the spot, but other pitches will need to be booked with the Cambridge Sports Pitch Booking Clerk ☎248229 (afternoons only).

Local clubs and societies for various sports and recreational hobbies will often welcome visitors. Details are available from the TIC and Public Library.

MULTI-SPORT FACILITIES

Kelsey Kerridge Sports Hall Gonville Place ☎68791. Large and small halls, squash courts, projectile gallery, etc. Bar and café. Day membership available, but advance booking advisable.

Sporturf Pitch, Abbey Sports Centre, Coldham's Common. Artificial grass pitch with floodlighting, changing rooms, showers, etc. Suitable for soccer and hockey, also five-a-side football, netball, cricket and tennis. Advance booking with Cambridge Sports Pitch Booking Clerk ☎ 248229 (afternoons).

Huntingdon Recreation Centre St Peter's Road ☎(0480) 54130. Swimming pool and two squash courts

Peterborough—Ferry Meadows, Nene Valley Park ☎ (0733) 234443. Watersports and other facilities.

St Ives—St Ivo Recreation Centre, Westwood Road ☎(0480) 64601. Sports hall, projectile hall, squash courts, bowling rinks, solarium

Wisbech—Hudson Sports Centre, Harecroft Road ☎(0945) 584230. Swimming pool, sports hall, bowling rinks

There are also Sports Centres at Bury St Edmunds, Ely, Great Dunmow, Mepal, Soham and Thetford

ANGLING

See under Fishing

BOARDSAILING

Peterborough Sailboard Club ☎(0733) 62858

BOAT HIRE

See Transport section

BOWLS

Greens at Alexandra Gardens, Barnwell Recreation Ground, Christ's Pieces, Coleridge Recreation Ground, Jesus Green, Lammas Land, Romsey Recreation Ground, Nightingale Avenue and King George V Recreation Ground.

CRICKET

First-class cricket matches held at Fenner's, the University cricket ground off Gresham Road.

Local club matches on Parker's Piece, and this and King George V Recreation Ground, Trumpington, available to hire.

FISHING

Rod licences for the Cam, the Ouse and tributary waters available from fishing tackle shops or Anglian Water Authority (Cambridge Division), Clarendon Road, Cambridge ☎61561. Permits also needed for some waters.

FOOTBALL (SOCCER)

Cambridge United (professional soccer club). Ground at Newmarket Road.

Pitches available at Abbey Sports Centre (Coldham's Common), Cherry Hinton Recreation Ground, Jesus Green, Trumpington and Chesterton Recreation Grounds.

Junior pitches at Coleridge and Nuns Way Recreation Grounds.

GOLF

Cambridgeshire Moat House Hotel Golf Club Bar Hill, nr Cambridge ☎Crafts Hill (0954) 80098 (18 hole Championship Course, undulating park with lake)

Girton Golf Club Dodford Lane, Girton ☎276169. Non-members Mon–Fri only, advance booking advisable (18 hole, parkland)

Gog Magog Golf Club
Babraham Road, Cambridge
☎247628. Users must be golf
club members or introduced
by a member of Gog Magog
Club, Mon–Fri only and
advance booking essential (18
hole and new 9 hole course)

Also golf clubs at Bury St
Edmunds, Downham Market,
Ely, Huntingdon, King's Lynn,
Newmarket, Peterborough,
Saffron Walden, St Neots,
Stowmarket, Sudbury,
Swaffham and Thetford.

HOCKEY

Pitches on Parker's Piece and
Jesus Green

HORSE-RACING

Newmarket—Racing Apr–
Oct. For details
☎(0638) 664151

PETANQUE (BOULES)

Abbey Sports Centre,
Coldham's Common

POINT TO POINT

Meetings at Cottenham and
Brampton. Contact TIC for
details

RIDING

Gransden Hall Riding School
Great Gransden (12m W
Cambridge) ☎(076 77) 366

Lodge Riding Stables Great
Abington (7m SE Cambridge)
☎891101

**Park House Stables Riding
School** Harston (6m SW
Cambridge) ☎870075

Miss Pickard's School New
Farm Stables, Bourn (8m W
Cambridge) ☎Caxton
(095 44) 501

Sawston Riding School
Common Lane Farm, Sawston
(6m S Cambridge) ☎835198

Mrs Turner Broadway Farm,
Lolworth (6m NW Cambridge)
☎Madingley (0954) 80159.
Facilities for the disabled

Windmill Stables Shepreth
Road, Barrington (7m SW
Cambridge) ☎871487

ROWING

University 'Bumps' held in Feb
and Jun (May Week), City
'Bumps' in Jul. Course
between Bait's Bite Lock,
Milton, and Stourbridge
Common. At other times of
year rowers may be seen
practising on the river from
Midsummer Common
northwards.
    'Leisure' rowing boats
available for hire—see under
Boat hire in Transport section.

RUGBY

University Rugby Union team
plays on first-class ground in
Grange Road.

SKATING

East of England Ice Rink
Mallard Road, Bretton, nr
Peterborough ☎(0733) 260222

Rollerbury Station Hill, Bury St
Edmunds (roller-skating)
☎(0284) 701215 (bookings),
701216 (management)

SWIMMING

Abbey Pool Coldham's
Common (open-air, heated,
summer only)

**Bottisham Village College
Pool** ☎Cambridge 811627 or
811934

Jesus Green (open-air,
summer only)

King's Hedges North Arbury
(bookable learner pool—
contact duty officer at
Parkside)

Parkside Pool Mill Road
☎350008. Indoor pool open
daily throughout year. Large
pool, learners' pool,
spectators' facilities, and
café

Sheep's Green (children's
pool, summer only)

Pools also available in a
number of other towns in the
area.

TENNIS

Major University matches
played at Fenner's, Gresham
Road.
    Courts at Jesus Green (hard
and grass) and Christ's Pieces
(hard)—charges made. Free
(hard) courts at Barnwell,
Lammas Land and Coleridge
and Nightingale Avenue
Recreation Grounds.

Shopping

The main city-centre shops in
Cambridge are situated in the
area between King's Parade/
Trinity Street and Sidney
Street/St Andrew's Street,
both north and south of
Market Street and in the Lion
Yard shopping centre. Major
chain stores, local department
stores and small specialist
shops are all well represented.
Early closing day is Thursday,
but most of the shops are
open six days a week. There is
a daily market in Market
Square which sells a wide
range of goods. Areas tending

to have a higher than average
concentration of a certain
type of shop include Trinity
Street for bookshops, Rose
Crescent for upmarket
clothes and gifts, and King's
Parade for gift shops. Away
from the centre other
shopping areas include the
new Grafton Centre (to the
east of the city centre) and
Mill Road.
    For advice on consumer
affairs contact the Consumer
Advice Centre, Central Library
☎311318. Open Mon–Fri
10–1 & 2–4.

EARLY CLOSING DAYS IN
SURROUNDING TOWNS

Bedford—Thu

Bury St Edmunds—Thu

Ely—Tue

King's Lynn—Wed

Newmarket—Wed

Peterborough—Mon/Thu

Saffron Walden—Thu

Stowmarket—Tue

Sudbury—Wed

Thaxted—Wed

Thetford—Wed

Wisbech—Wed

ANTIQUE SHOPS IN CAMBRIDGE

In addition to the following shops, the market usually has some stalls selling bric-à-brac and antiques.

Antiques Etcetera 18 King Street ☎62825

Jess Applin 8 Lensfield Road ☎315168

John Beazor & Sons Ltd 78 & 80 Regent Street ☎355178

Buckies 31 Trinity Street ☎357910

The Cabin 95a Ditton Walk ☎242029

Malcolm C Clark 3 Pembroke Street ☎357117

Collectors Market Dales Brewery, Gwydir Street—antiques and bric-à-brac. Open Mon–Fri 9.30–5, Sat 9.30–5.30

Collins & Clarke 81 Regent Street ☎353801

Cottage Antiques 16–18 Lensfield Road ☎316698

Dolphin Antiques 33 Trumpington Street ☎354180

Gabor Cossa Antiques 34 Trumpington Street ☎356049

King Street Collections 56a King Street ☎312015

Lensfield Antiques 12 Lensfield Road ☎357636

Dorothy Radford 132 Shelford Road, Trumpington ☎840179

S J Webster–Speakmann 79 Regent Street ☎315048

Willroy of Dales Dales Brewery, Gwydir Street ☎311687

BOOKSHOPS

In addition to the bookshops listed below, the market often has stalls selling publishers' remainders and secondhand books, and there are regular bookfairs in the Guildhall and Fisher Hall (details from TIC).

The Bookroom 13a St Eligius Street ☎69694 (antiquarian)

The Bookshop 24 Magdalene Street ☎62457 (secondhand)

Browne's Bookstore 56 Mill Road ☎350968 (new & secondhand)

Cambridge International Book Centre 42 Hills Road ☎65400 (paperbacks, especially English for foreign students)

G R David 3 & 16 St Edward's Passage ☎354619 (remainders, secondhand & antiquarian)

Deighton Bell & Co 13 Trinity Street ☎353939/60791 (antiquarian & secondhand)

Galloway & Porter 30 Sidney Street ☎67876 (new & secondhand); 3 Green Street ☎67876 (antiquarian & secondhand)

Grapevine Bookshop Unit 6, Dales Brewery, Gwydir Street ☎61808 (radical progressive literature)

The Green Street Bookshop 5 Green Street ☎68088 (religions, philosophy, history & history of science)

The Haunted Bookshop St Edward's Passage ☎312913 (antiquarian)

W Heffer & Sons 20 Trinity Street ☎358351 (very large stock of new books); 30 Trinity Street ☎356200 (children's books); 13 Trinity Street ☎61815 (paperbacks); 31 St Andrew's Street ☎354778 (paperbacks); 22 The Grafton Centre ☎313117 (new incl children's)

A R Mowbray 14 King's Parade ☎358452 (mainly religious)

Quinto 34 Trinity Street ☎358279 (antiquarian & secondhand)

Scripture Union Book Shop 88a Regent Street ☎352727 (religious)

Sherratt & Hughes 1 Trinity Street ☎355488 (new incl academic)

W H Smith & Son 26 Lion Yard ☎311313 (new)

CRAFT SHOPS AND WORKSHOPS IN CAMBRIDGE

All Saints Churchyard All Saints Passage (off St John's Street), open-air craft market Fri & Sat in Jun, Jul & Aug

Brass Rubbing Centre St Giles' Church, Castle Street ☎61318.

Open Tue–Sat 10–5 & Mon in Jul & Aug

Cobble Yard Craft Centre Napier Street, off Newmarket Road (various craft workshops)

Fisher Hall Craft Market (nr TIC). Markets every Sat throughout the year, also Fri in Jul and Thu & Fri in Aug. ☎Ely (0353) 740725 for details

Scotts Bindery 53 Panton Street ☎64862 (bookbinding)

CRAFT SHOPS AND WORKSHOPS OUTSIDE CAMBRIDGE

The shops and workshops listed below are only a selection of those to be found in the area and have been chosen because they are generally open to visitors during normal working hours. However, in all cases it is advisable to telephone first to check opening times, exact location and the items available.

Buckden—L'Bidi Studio, 81 High Street ☎(0480) 810545. See under St Ives

Bury St Edmunds—Barrow Pottery, 27 The Green, Barrow (6m W Bury) ☎(0284) 810961

Bury St Edmunds—Clare Craft Pottery, Windy Ridge, Broom Hill Lane, Woolpit (8m E Bury) ☎Elmswell (0359) 41277

Bury St Edmunds—Craft at the Suffolk Barn, Fornham Road, Great Barton ☎Great Barton (028 487) 317 (wide range of crafts for sale—open mid Mar–Dec)

Bury St Edmunds—Elm Tree Cottage Gallery, Gedding Road, Drinkstone Green, nr Bury St Edmunds ☎Rattlesden (044 93) 366

Castle Hedingham The Pottery, 37 St James' Street ☎Halstead (0787) 60036

Ely—Steeplegate Ltd, 16–18 High Street ☎(0353) 4731 (gifts and craft gallery)

Houghton—Alice Green Crafts, Monument House, Thicket Road ☎Huntingdon (0480) 300977 (flower jewellery and pyrography plus other crafts in shop)

Ickleton—David & Jean Whitaker, Frogge Cottage, 48 Frogge Street ☎Saffron Walden (0799) 30304 (furniture makers and wood turners)

Little Abington—Abington Pottery, 26 High Street ☎ 891723

Mildenhall—Kohl & Son, 2 Finchley Avenue, Industrial Estate ☎(0638) 712069 (leather goods)

Royston—Foxhall Studio, Kelshall, nr Royston ☎Kelshall (076 387) 209 (stained-glass windows and other items)

St Ives—John Britton Hand-Engraved Glass, 9 Bridge Street ☎(0480) 61065

St Ives—Gem Gardens Glass Art, 18 East Street, Robb's Yard ☎(0480) 301660

St Ives—L'Bidi Studio, 40 The Broadway ☎(0480) 66886 (hand-painted silk goods made and sold together with other craft goods; also gallery displaying work by local artists)

Sawston (6m S Cambridge)—Eastern Counties Sheepskin Tannery Shop ☎834757

Somersham Pottery 3 & 4 West Newlands nr Huntingdon ☎Ramsey (Cambs) (0487) 841823 (stoneware, terracotta and porcelain)

Stilton—Chestnut Country Crafts, 93 North Street ☎Peterborough (0733) 240636 or 240016 (shop selling East Anglian crafts)

Stowmarket—Combs Tannery Shop (1½m S) ☎(0449) 674656

Stowmarket—Museum of East Anglian Life ☎(0449) 612229. See Places to Visit section for opening hours

Thaxted—Glendale Forge, Monk Street, nr Thaxted ☎(0371) 830466 (blacksmiths)

Thurston—Mulden End Studio, Unit 7, Thurston Granary (nr Bury St Edmunds) ☎Pakenham (0359) 32082 (hand-painted ceramic buildings)

Welney Craft Centre Croft House, Main Street, Welney, Wisbech ☎Welney (035 471) 238 (various East Anglian crafts for sale)

Whittlesey—The Craft Shop/ Whittlesey Miniatures, 6 St Mary's Street ☎Peterborough (0733) 203620 (miniature figurines and various other craft items)

Willingham—Cambridge Stained Glass, 10 George Street ☎(0954) 60301

DEPARTMENT STORES

Co-op Burleigh Street ☎358844

Debenhams Grafton Centre ☎353525

Eaden Lilley 10 Market Street ☎358822

Marks and Spencer 6 Sidney Street ☎355219

Robert Sayle St Andrew's Street ☎61292

Joshua Taylor Sidney Street & Bridge Street ☎314151

Woolworths 13 Sidney Street ☎357168

FOOD

Cakes and chocolates:
Fitzbillies 52 Trumpington Street ☎352500.
Also at 50 Regent Street and Eaden Lilley, Market Street

Delicatessens:
Adams 13 St John's Street ☎350722; 26 Mill Road ☎353013

Cambridge Continental 9 The Broadway, Mill Road ☎248069

Country Gourmet 84 High Street, Great Shelford ☎845081

Jason's Shop 16 Milton Road ☎68735

Spencer Stores 33 Hills Road ☎60230

Health/Wholefood shops:
Arjuna 12 Mill Road ☎64845

Beaumonts Heaith Store Grafton Centre ☎314544

Health Food Store 3 Rose Crescent ☎353305

Holland & Barrett 4 Bradwell's Court ☎68914

Natural Selection 30 Regent Street ☎65819

NEWSAGENTS

See Useful Information section

PHOTOGRAPHY— QUICK FILM DEVELOPMENT

See Useful Information section

PRINTS/PICTURES/ ART REPRODUCTIONS

Athena Reproductions Ltd 19 Lion Yard ☎69890

Benet Gallery 19 King's Parade ☎353783

Cambridge Fine Art 33 Church Street, Little Shelford ☎842866

Cambridge Holographics 29 Magdalene Street ☎311322

Jean Pain 7 King's Parade ☎313970

Transport

AA CENTRES

24hr-breakdown service ☎312302. Other AA details are listed in the Useful Information section

AIR TRAVEL

Cambridge Airport Newmarket Road ☎61133. Tours and charter flights handled by Premier Airlines

Ltd ☎Teversham (022 05) 3621. Air taxi services operated by Midas Ltd ☎Teversham (022 05) 3804 and Cecil Aviation Ltd ☎359674

Stansted Airport (just over ½hr drive down M11 from Cambridge). ☎Bishop's Stortford (0279) 57641 or ☎502379

BICYCLE HIRE

Bicycles are by far the most convenient means of transport in Cambridge. But if your cycling is 'rusty', do practice on a quiet back-street first!

Armada Cycle 45a Suez Road ☎210421

H Drake 58 Hills Road ☎63468

Geoff's Bike Hire 65 Devonshire Road ☎65629

J Hart 82 Colville Road ☎244533

Ben Hayward & Son Laundress Lane ☎352294

Howes Cycles 104 Regent Street ☎350350

W J Ison 72 Chesterton Road ☎315845

N J Thake Cycles 163–167 Mill Road ☎214999

University Cycles 9 Victoria Avenue ☎355517

BOAT HIRE

The boatyards, situated at Mill Lane (by Mill Pond) and at Quayside (near Magdalene Street Bridge) are open Etr to early Oct. From Mill Lane punts, rowing boats and canoes can be taken either along the Backs or upriver to Grantchester; from Quayside they are available for the Backs only.

Punting is not as easy as it sometimes looks, and visitors may prefer to hire a chauffeurpunt. Details available from TIC.

BRITISH RAIL

Station in Station Road to south-east of city centre. Passenger enquiries ☎311999 (Mon–Sat 7.30am–9.30pm, Sun 8.30am–9.30pm). Travel Centre open 5.30am–10.30pm (Continental Booking 9–5.30 Mon–Sat). 24hr recorded timetable with details of main trains to and from London ☎359602. Parcel enquiries ☎69169,

freight services ☎358800. Trains run approx hourly to both Liverpool Street and King's Cross in London (change at Royston on the latter service).

British Transport Police ☎352031

Stations outside Cambridge: Bury St Edmunds ☎(0284) 3947

Ely (c/o Cambridge ☎311999)

Huntingdon ☎(0480) 54468

King's Lynn ☎(0553) 772021

Peterborough ☎(0733) 68181

BUS AND COACH SERVICES

Cambus Ltd Cowley Road ☎321544. Inquiry Office at Drummer Street Bus Station open Mon–Sat, 8.30–5.30 ☎355554. Also hire out 16-seater minibuses with driver ☎69578

National Express ☎460711

Premier Travel Services Drummer Street ☎353333

CAR HIRE

A number of the firms listed below, indicated (ch), have children's car seats available. These should generally be booked in advance.

Avis Rent-A-Car 243 Mill Road ☎212551 (ch)

Budget Rent-A-Car Newmarket Road ☎323838 (ch)

Tim Brinton Cars Ltd (Peugeot), 147 Hills Road ☎213221

CamKars Hire 362 Milton Road ☎65706

Gilbert Rice Ltd 350 Newmarket Road ☎315435

Godfrey Davis Car & Van Hire 315/345 Mill Road ☎248198 (ch)

Hertz (see Willhire)

Kenning Car Hire 47 Coldham's Lane ☎61538 (ch)

Marshalls Car Hire Jesus Lane ☎62211

Renorent West's Garage, Newmarket Road ☎351616

Swan National Car Rental 264 Newmarket Road ☎65438

F Vindis & Sons High Street, Sawston (6m S Cambridge) ☎833110 (ch)

Willhire Ltd (Hertz), 41 High Street, Chesterton ☎68888

CAR PARKING

Mon–Sat (ex BH) between 8.30am and 6.30pm street parking in central controlled parking zone only at metered parking bays.

Short-stay car parks at Lion Yard (multi-storey), Park Street (multi-storey), Grafton Centre (two multi-storey—one entered from Maid's Causeway, one from East Road)

Long-stay car parks are to be found at Gonville Place (multi-storey), Saxon Street and Gold Street

Coach park City Football Ground, Milton Road

PETROL—24HR GARAGES

Four Went Ways Self Serve Little Abington (7m SW Cambridge) ☎Cambridge 835677

PUNT HIRE

See under Boat hire

RAIL SERVICES

See under British Rail

TAXIS

Taxi ranks at Station (24hr), and 7am–2am at Drummer Street, Market Hill and St Andrew's Street (by Robert Sayles)

All the following taxi firms are open at least 7am–7pm with those indicated (24hr) always open

Al Taxis ☎359123 (24hr)

ABC Taxis ☎244444 (24hr)

Able Cars ☎213232 (24hr)

ACE Taxis ☎244469

Brown's Taxis & Private Hire ☎833927

CABCO ☎312444

CAMTAX ☎313131 (24hr)

Intercity Taxis ☎312233 (24hr)

S & H Taxis ☎314314 (24hr)

United Taxis ☎352222 (24hr)

Useful Information

AA

Cambridge—AA 24hr-breakdown service ☎312302. Travel shop 46/48 St Andrew's Street ☎66895 (insurance) 65613 (travel agency)

Other AA 24hr-breakdown service nos:

Bedford (0234) 218888

King's Lynn (0553) 773731

ADVICE CENTRES

Citizens' Advice Bureau 2 Pike's Walk ☎356442/353875 Open Mon 9.30–6, Tue–Fri 9.30–4.30, Sat 10–12

Consumer Advice Centre—see Shopping section

BANKS

All the banks listed are open Mon–Fri 9.30–3.30. Barclays and the Midland are open longer hours and the TSB is open until 6pm Fri. On the Sat the following banks are open: Barclays, Market Hill, 9.30–12; Midland, Market Hill, 9.30–12.30; Lloyds, Sidney Street, 10.00–3; National Westminster, St Andrew's Street, 9.30–12.30.

Barclays:
15 Bene't Street
92 Cherry Hinton Road
28 Chesterton Road
30 Market Hill
58 Mill Road
76 Newmarket Road
35 Sidney Street

Co-operative Bank:
Burleigh Street

Lloyds:
78 Cherry Hinton Road
Chesterton Road
Lloyds House, Regent Street
90a Mill Road
70 Newmarket Road
95 Regent Street
3 Sidney Street
36 Trinity Street

Midland:
13 Burleigh Street
62 Cherry Hinton Road
58 Chesterton Road
62 Hills Road
32 Market Hill
52 St Andrew's Street
7 The Broadway, Mill Road

National Westminster:
10 Bene't Street
37 Fitzroy Street
56 St Andrew's Street
26 Trinity Street

Royal Bank of Scotland:
28 Trinity Street

Trustee Savings Bank (TSB):
26 Burleigh Street
6 Jesus Lane
224 Mill Road
6 St Andrew's Street

BUREAUX DE CHANGE

See also Banks listed above.

Abbott's Travel Agency 25 Sidney Street ☎351636

Thomas Cook & Son Travel Agency 5 Market Hill ☎66141

DRY CLEANERS AND LAUNDERETTES

Dry cleaners:
Sketchley Cleaners 16 Lion Yard & 7 Bradwell's Court

Smiths Cleaners 5a Burleigh Street & 20 St Andrew's Street

Swiss Laundry Ltd Cherry Hinton Road

Launderettes:
1 Arbury Court
115 High Street, Chesterton
28 King Street
161 Mill Road
5 Rectory Terrace, Cherry Hinton
12 Victoria Avenue

EMERGENCY

Fire, Police & Ambulance—dial 999 and tell the Operator which service you require

Samaritans (24hr service for suicidal and despairing)—1 Parker Street ☎64455

Services:
Electricity—☎61266 (24hr)

Gas—☎61234 or Peterborough (0733) 68911 (office hours), Freefone 286 or Potters Bar (0707) 51234 (after office hours)

Water—Cambridge Water Company (water supply), Rustat Road ☎247351 (24hr service). Anglian Water Authority, Clarendon Road,

Cambridge ☎61561. Emergency calls outside office hours. ☎Stoke Ferry (0366) 500687

GUIDED TOURS

A variety of guided tour services are available from the TIC (☎322640) and are summarised below:

Individual tours—daily walking tours, generally lasting about 2hrs and visiting the major colleges (and where possible King's College Chapel). Tickets should be purchased between 24 and ½hr before the start of the tours which depart from the TIC at the following times. Mon–Sat (Apr–May, 11 & 2, Jun–mid Jun, 11, 1 & 2, mid Jun–Sep, 11, 1, 2 & 3); Sun (Apr–Sep as weekdays but 11.15 rather than 11); Mon–Sat (Oct, 11, 1 & 2, Nov, 2); Dec–Mar Sat (only) 2

Historic Cambridge Tours Jul & Aug daily at 6.30; also Drama Tours (details on request)

Group tours—private tours of the colleges and historical sites, and tours based on a variety of themes (e.g. archaeology and anthropology, education, literature and libraries, royal Cambridge) can be arranged. PLEASE NOTE THAT ANY GROUP OF TEN OR MORE PERSONS WISHING TO VISIT THE COLLEGES MUST BE ACCOMPANIED BY A BLUE BADGED CAMBRIDGE GUIDE

Guided tours also take place in Bury St Edmunds, Ely & King's Lynn. Contact local TIC for details.

HEALTH

Chemists—details of late-night opening are generally listed in the local papers or are available from doctors' surgeries.

Dentists, doctors and opticians are listed in the Yellow Pages telephone directory, and most will provide emergency treatment. If you are unable to find one willing to help contact the Family Practitioner Service ☎242731.

Hospitals (24hr accident and emergency):

Cambridge—Addenbrooke's Hospital, Hills Road ☎245151

Ely—Royal Air Force Hospital, Lynn Road ☎(0353) 5781

Huntingdon—Hinching-brooke Hospital, Hinching-brooke Park ☎(0480) 56131

LIBRARIES & RECORDS OFFICE

Central Library Lion Yard ☎65252. Lending library and Cambridgeshire Collection (local studies) open Mon–Fri 9.30–6, Sat 9.30–5; reference library open Mon–Fri 9–7, Sat 9–5; exhibition room open Mon–Sat 9–5

Suburban libraries at Arbury Court, Cherry Hinton (High Street), Mill Road, Milton Road (Ascham Road), Newmarket Road and Rock Road

Cambridgeshire Records Office Shire Hall ☎317281. Open Mon–Fri 9–12.45, 1.45–5.15 (or 4.15 Fri) and by appt Tue 5.15–9pm

NEWSAGENTS

Adams & Dellar 77 Regent Street

Bridge 18 Magdalene Street

Burleigh Newsagents 42 Burleigh Street

Castle Street Newsagents 4 Castle Street

City Newspapers 8 Market Passage

The Corner Shop 251 Chesterton Road

Douglas & Wilson 301 Mill Road

Forbuoys 1 Adkins Corner, Perne Road, 41 Arbury Court & 132 Wulfstan Way

Grey Davis News 41 Trumpington Street

Kings Newsagents 214 Mill Road

Lambert & Ward 46 Hills Road

Lavells Ltd 72 Mill Road

NSS Newsagents 108 Cherry Hinton Road & 11 Victoria Avenue

Newnham Newsagents 38 Newnham Road

Nicholsons Whites News 115 Perne Road

M & S Orbell 22 Victoria Road

Rossendale The Kiosk, Fitzroy Street

W H Smith 26 Lion Yard & Railway Station

Stops Shops Newsagents 84 Campkin Road, 239 Cherry Hinton Road, 158 Hills Road & 279 Newmarket Road

Uff 109 Milton Road

United News 18 Bradwell's Court

Vinery News 1 Vinery Way

Whites News 12 King's Parade

NEWSPAPERS

Cambridge Evening News & Cambridge Weekly News, 51 Newmarket Road ☎358877

Town Crier Unit 1, The Techno Park, Newmarket Road ☎69966

PHOTOGRAPHY—QUICK FILM DEVELOPMENT

AM Photographic 31 Clifton Road ☎213271 (2–3hr)

Anglia Photoworks 66 Devonshire Road ☎355998 (film in by 10.30am, ready by 5pm)

The Cambridge Photographers 4 Hills Road ☎62857 (approx 24hr service)

Colourquick Ltd 58 Regent Street ☎69291 (film in by 9am, ready midday; in after midday, ready next day)

Photolab Express c/o Boots the Chemist, 28 Petty Cury ☎68580 (1hr & 24hr service)

United Photofinishers Ltd 36 Humberstone Road ☎65651 (film in by 4pm, ready next day at 10am)

POLICE STATIONS

Cambridge—Parkside ☎358966

Ely—Nutholt Lane ☎(0353) 2392

Huntingdon—Ferrars Road ☎(0480) 56111

POST OFFICES

Main Post Office 9–11 St Andrew's Street ☎351212. Open Mon–Fri 9–5.30, Sat 9–1. Last collection Mon–Fri 7.45.
Also 23–24 Trinity Street and elsewhere in suburbs of city

Sorting Office Mill Road. Last collection Mon–Fri 7.30, Sat 1

RADIO (LOCAL STATIONS)

Hereward Radio ☎Peterborough (0733) 46225. Broadcast on 1332kHz (225m), VHF 102.7MHz

Radio Cambridgeshire ☎315970. Broadcast (South Cambs) on 1449kHz (207m), VHF 103.9MHz, and (North Cambs) on 1026kHz (292m), VHF 96MHz

Radio Saxon ☎Bury St Edmunds (0284) 701511. Broadcast on 1251kHz (240m), VHF 96.4MHz

TOILETS

Those toilets indicated (d) are accessible to disabled people in wheelchairs

Alexandra Gardens (off Carlyle Road)

Chesterton Road (d)

Drummer Street (d)

Grafton Centre

Jesus Green (nr footbridge to Chesterton Road)

Lion Yard (d)—near library

Newnham Road (Lammas Land)

Northampton Street

Park Street Car Park (d)

Parker's Piece (Gonville Place)

Quayside (d)

TOURIST INFORMATION CENTRES

Cambridge—Wheeler Street ☎322640. Open all year Mon–Fri 9–5.30 (9–6 Mar–Oct, 9–7 Jul & Aug), Sat 9–5; May–Sep Sun & BH (10.30–3.30). Closed Good Fri, Chr & New Year

Bury St Edmunds—Abbey Gardens, Angel Hill ☎(0284) 64667. Open early May—Sep Mon—Fri 9—5.30, Sat 10—4.30; Jul & Aug only Sun 10—12. During winter months information available from Thingoe House, Northgate Street ☎(0284) 63233 ext 427 (Mon—Thu 9—5.20, Fri 9—4.25)

Ely—The Library, Palace Green ☎(0353) 2062. Open Mon (10—7), Tue (10—5), Wed, Thu (10—6), Fri (10—7), Sat (9.30—5); & Sun & BH 12—4 (Jun—Sep)

Huntingdon—The Library, Princes Street ☎(0480) 425831. Open Oct—Mar Mon—Fri 10—6, Sat 9—5; Apr—Sep Mon—Fri 9.30—5.30, Sat 9—5. Open summer BH

King's Lynn—The Old Goal House, Saturday Market Place ☎(0553) 763044. Open all year Mon—Fri 10—5 (or 4.30 Fri); also May—Oct Sat 10—4

Lavenham—The Guildhall, Market Place ☎(0787) 248207. Open Apr—Sep daily 10—5

Peterborough—Town Hall, Bridge Street ☎(0733) 63141. Open all year Mon—Fri 9—5; Jun—Aug Sat 10—1. Also Central Library, Broadway ☎(0733) 48343 ext 36. Open all year Mon—Fri 10—7 (5pm Thu), Sat 9.30—5. Closed BH Mon & Tue

Saffron Walden—Corn Exchange, Market Square ☎(0799) 24282. Open all year (ex BH) Mon—Sat 9.30—4.30 (Nov—Mar 10—4)

Sudbury—Public Library, Market Hill ☎(0787) 72092. Open Tue, Thu & Sat 9.30—5, Wed 9.30—1, Fri 9.30—7.30

Thetford—Ancient House Museum, White Hart Street ☎(0842) 2599. Open all year (ex Good Fri & 25—26 Dec), Mon 10—1 & 2—5, Tue—Sat 10—5; also Sun 2—5 (late May—late Sep only)

Wisbech—District Library, Ely Place ☎(0945) 583263. Open all year Tue & Wed 10—6, Thu & Fri 10—7, Sat 9.30—5

Pocket Guide
AA
INDEX

Main entries are shown in **bold**
Entries for places outside the city of Cambridge generally refer
to 'places of interest' listed in the Directory section

Opening
doors to
the World
of books

**Book
Tokens**

Book Tokens
can be
bought and
exchanged
at most
bookshops